"There aren't too many writers who share struggles like a skillful Sherpa leading the reader on a journey to the blast radius of Jesus. Kevin's stories do just this and equally as important, he connects us to our own. In "Can You Trust Me This Much?", Kevin helps us see the events of today and even those in our past-the good, the bad and the scary-as nudges of The Spirit. All of it coming together to move us closer to the version of the person Jesus is sculpting us to be."

– BOB GOFF
New York Times bestselling author of *Love Does,*
Dream Big, and *Undistracted*

"Kevin Lewis is a truth teller, even when the truth requires uncomfortable courage. *Can You Trust Me This Much?* is a story with big laughs, ugly cries, and real life. This book is a refreshing, relentless reminder of just how much we are loved and that we are not ever alone."

– KIMBERLY STUART
Author of *Sugar: A Novel* and the *Heidi Elliott* series.

"Kevin was an athlete, a coach, a teacher, a Christian rapper and a small business owner who grew up the only boy with four sisters. And that's just part of his story!

His witty, amusing stories draw the reader in, as he shares not only the variety of his adventures, but what God was doing in the process. I never played his sports or experienced his role models, but his details bring them to life and I found myself reminiscing about the pivotal people from my life.

Kevin reminds us that the journey of faith is not all sunshine and rainbows. But even in those moments of questioning we can find courage and hope."

– STEPHANIE NELSON
Founder CouponMom.com and
Author, *Imagine More: Do What You Love,*
Discover Your Potential (October 2023)

"We all have our "hard." If we aren't in it, we may be heading for it or just came out of it. Whether that's an unexpected diagnosis. The death of a loved one. The loss of a job. A divorce. Or in Kevin's case, a mass shooting that occurred in his tiny town. Hards are all around us.

In "Can You Trust Me This Much?", and through Kevin's life experiences, he reminds us that all God asks from us is to have faith the size of a tiny, almost microscopic, mustard seed. He has an amazing way of connecting with the reader and through his incredible (and often hilarious) storytelling, he encourages us that even through the hard, trusting God, even just "this much" is always enough."

– BRANDON JANOUS
Author, *Just Do!: Stories about Discovering*
Purpose Gaining Perspective and Being Present

Publishing Assistance by
B&T Publishing Services
Knoxville, TN • Nashville, TN

First printing, June 2023

Library of Congress Cataloging-In-Publication Data
Lewis, Kevin
    Can You Trust Me This Much?: Finding Hope, Courage and Purpose in the Gentle (and
    Sometimes Jarring) Nudges of the Spirit
Kevin Lewis — 1st ed.
    p. cm.
    Includes bibliographical references.
    ISBN: 979-8-9880165-1-9 / 979-8-9880165-2-6
    1. Biography 2. Inspiration

Cover Design & Interior Layout by Tim Marshall
Printed in China

Can you trust me this much?

Finding Hope, Courage and Purpose in the Gentle *(and Sometimes Jarring)* Nudges of the Spirit.

KEVIN LEWIS

Contents

Dedication

Occasionally simple words scribbled out as a prayer become something far more than we can ever imagine. When the wheels are falling off in life, it's easy to return to prayer. At one such point I scribbled down the words, "Can you trust me this much?" In the spice drawer I found mustard seeds and scotch-taped one on each note. I had about a dozen of these notes and randomly taped them up as reminders. They were on my computer screens, my bathroom mirror and even the dashboard of my vehicle had one of these "spiritual check engine" lights. Not because I was super holy, but because I was honestly struggling to have that much faith. I needed the reminders. All my energies were directed at fixing, saving and keeping it all on track. I didn't want to concede that maybe God had something different planned. If you've experienced anything similar, this book is dedicated to you.

● ● ●

It's also dedicated to the children and families of Buffalo, Minnesota. It's for all the gymnasts, dancers, karate students and ninjas I had the pleasure of meeting during my time there. It was an honor to be a small part of your life and community. I am especially thankful for having experienced how our small town bonded and came together after the events of February 9, 2021. While this story started there, it is much bigger.

●　　　●　　　●

This book is also dedicated to you, the reader. In this life, each of us experiences hurt. For some, it's early in life and for others it comes later. For many, we experience doses of hurt at various points along the way. But we have a choice. We can deny the hurt. We can attempt to minimize, compartmentalize it, and keep it in a box. It's a natural reaction. Because the hurts can leave us feeling isolated and alone. We think, talking about it won't help or no one can understand what has happened. But Jesus calls us to more.

Jesus gave us prayer as a means to converse with His Father. If you've ever wondered, If there is a loving God, how, why are these things allowed to happen then I encourage you to keep reading. I know in my own life when I've experienced those questions sometimes my conversing with God has slipped over to shouting matches. But we can be encouraged. Jesus experienced hurts too. It's only when we are brave enough to dive into our hurts and questions that we can really know our kinship to Jesus. The point is not to dwell deep beneath the oceans of hurt or to play a victim role. Still, we need to probe and in our seeking, we find others with adjacent stories. It's there that Jesus meets us. He intertwines the broken hurt pieces together to serve His purpose. In exploring our questions of "how" and "why," we learn purpose.

It is not easy work. It does not take away the hurt we know. But when we are open to doing the hard work, God silences the screaming voices and reminds us we are not alone. It's here He uses our hurts to teach us compassion, mercy, grace. And most importantly, the ability to freely give those things away. In doing so, the hurts we've known are bound with those Jesus knew and genuine healing can begin.

An Introduction

I've spent the majority of my life not talking about these things. We learned from an early age to not be whiners or complainers. We were taught by coaches and parents and even by our faith to be tough and persevere. "Suck it up"; "Keep going"; "Man it up, Buttercup"; and "Don't you dare quit on me!" were all battle cries to persist.

On February 9, 2021, a mass shooting took place in Buffalo, Minnesota. It was just 1.2 miles from the children's activity center I owned and operated. As tough as I'd learned to be, no coach mantra was going to help on this day. I had cleaned the bathrooms and emptied the cubbies. Rainbow-sparkle Crocs, a leopard-print hair scrunchy, and a Batman water bottle were newly lost, hoping-to-be-found items. I learned schools were in lock-down and instantly thought of all the teachers, student aides, and school administrators who brought their children to us for lessons. I thought of the police officers and emergency responders who also had children in our programs. And of course, I thought of the students, the little kids we did all of this for. I wondered if I knew someone who was hurt. Or worse.

I thought back to my days of hiding under desks or in locker rooms for tornado drills. No tornado ever came. But on this day the kids I coached really did hide under their desks. Teachers moved from drill to real life as they barricaded classrooms. Meanwhile, employees and parents called and emailed the gym, all asking if we would be opened or closed. Soon the news helicopter flew above. I couldn't help but see it as out of place. It's the kind of thing you only see when they chase down bad guys on television.

Still not sure of what to do, I recalled the podcast I'd stumbled upon the night before. The takeaway was "when extraordinary things occur, just do extra of the ordinary things to help make sense of it." I decided to send an email to the host of the podcast and his guest. I'd never met them, but I thought asking them to pray would be one additional, ordinary thing I could do this day. Eventually we got the all-clear, and I decided fear could not win. If only for those little ones, come hell or high water, we would provide a single sliver of normal for them this day.

It was a Tuesday, and this meant my ninja night. The first class was my little ones, the three- to five-year-olds. I always started my classes with a goofy question, like "If Mom let you pick dinner for your house tonight, what would your family be eating?" After the silly answers of pizza, peanut butter and jelly, and boogers, I reminded them to get their shoes and socks off. That's when a five-year-old boy raised his hand. This little guy looked me in the eye and matter-of-factly asked, "Did you hear about the man who took the gun and shot the people dead?"

No amount of formal training or just being human had prepared me to hear, or attempt to answer, his question. Until this day all the shooting and killing I'd heard about was in the news, always safely removed and far enough away. But this time the police helicopter had flown over my business. People I knew had hidden in fear. And this little kid right in front of me was asking questions no five-year-old ever should.

We made it through the evening despite some fears and a few tears. Only one child was absent from my classes. His mom was a county 911 dispatcher and his dad a sheriff's deputy. They'd had a busy day. Overwhelmingly parents and kids were so appreciative with verbal and even a few unspoken thank-yous for holding classes. While we'd done the right thing, the events of the day would forever change each of us as our small town became the next to be strong. For this day, I was thankful; to be connected to this community, to all of law enforcement, for the courage of my dedicated staff, and for the not-so-easy decision to hold classes.

●　　●　　●

Lying in bed that night, I'm sure I wasn't the only one thinking about the horrific events of the day. I knew we'd learn more in the days to come. But right then, I found myself haunted by the five-year-old ninja. His words took me back to when I was his age. I reconnected to five-year-old me. I spent the rest of the night reliving scary, scarring events of the past four and a half decades. I cried, filling a pillow with tears. Older me was full of a thousand versions of the questions: If there is a living, loving God, if His Son really came to be among us, if He really breathed His Holy Spirit over us, then how did all these things happen?

Not sleeping, I rolled over to check email. I'd received what I thought was an auto-reply to the email I'd sent earlier in the day. To my surprise, it was the podcast host. He had no clue who I was and likely had never heard of Buffalo, Minnesota. He assured me of his prayers for our town and then encouraged me to be taking notes. He said I might have a book or two in me. What? How did he know? Had he been a part of the day? Had he somehow known what I'd relived with younger me?

I got out of bed and started writing all of this down. I accepted I might not get the answers to the questions I've spent the majority of my life not allowing myself to ask, talk or even think about. I understand hurts and bad things happen and they don't come with easy answers, at least not on this side of heaven. I also figured out I am not alone, I hadn't been abandoned, forgotten, or discarded. I was gently reminded that the God who at times seems so very far away, disconnected, and unconcerned, is actually very present and intimately aware. God has seen it all and is at work bringing good out of whatever the universe throws our way.

•　　•　　•

The following Chapters are filled with my stories, but I am not the hero of this book—Jesus is. I don't presume the events of my life are more special or traumatic than yours. In fact, I know too many who have had it far worse. I invite you into each story and trust you to walk alongside present me and younger me. Each Chapter is a true, real-life adventure in which the advocate Jesus left for us walks alongside, nudges, and asks the question, "Can you trust me this much?" What we can find is the smallest seed, a reminder of lessons learned through each experience. They are nourished by the tears, the muck and the mire that is our life. Beyond the specific events of our story is the seed of what Jesus has done and is doing.

Together let's not be afraid to press into our wounds. It's OK, Jesus invited Thomas to do the same. Maybe, like me, you've built a house, moved in, and made a monument to your hurts. We are called to do more than this. Let's walk together, discover, learn, unlearn, and relearn those things He is doing anew. Let us go boldly into those deep dark places, knowing He is working all things out and bringing us up for fresh air.

We've all wondered aloud, "How does a loving God allow this to happen?" when the mass shootings and natural disasters happen. And perhaps to a lesser degree when we see personal struggles, the ones we all go through: loss of jobs, friends, family, watching friends struggle or die from horrific ailments, miscarriages, and endings that didn't go the way we'd hoped they would. We've all been there. We've all experienced something. But the hurt we experienced might have been one of those gentle nudges asking if we really do trust.

The tensions between what we say we believe and what we experience in real time can skew our faith. But Jesus is right there, taking our hand, inviting us in, calling us to follow Him. He said, "My grace is sufficient for you," and maybe, like me, you've stopped or been distracted by the current situation. But Jesus didn't stop. The second part of what He said provides us hope: "[because] my power is made perfect in weakness." We can have hope in our moments of weakness, our questions of doubt. Paul responded to this concept by saying, "So therefore, I will boast about my weaknesses, so that His power may rest on me. That is why, for Christ's sake, I delight in weaknesses, in insults, in hardships, in persecutions, in difficulties. For when I am weak, then I am strong."

My intent is not to boast about how messed up my life has been. I'm not trying to impress or disgust you, nor to glorify our struggles. Rather, I think we'll find our stories are more similar than different. And there is a shared hope and strength to be found. Like any journey, this will take us through some dark valleys and up to some pretty awesome peaks. The going isn't easy, but we all know sometimes the road less taken is well worth it. Along the way we will have a chance to breathe, reflect, and remind ourselves that no matter how dire or dark the day may seem, He is the Good Shepherd. He longs to pick us up, carry us on His shoulders, and bring us back. They say, "a cord of three strands doesn't easily break." I am counting on you, me, and that guy at the back of the boat. Let's go.

CHAPTER 1

"All Aboard!"

There is something fascinating about the loud cry from train conductors in the movies. You know the ones depicting a time when traveling by train was normal. The surge of activity, the uniformed official attempting to get travelers on the train in an orderly, timely fashion. The rumblings and steam of the engines could fill a space with thick fog. We know it's hard to see in a fog—be it from a train, the fog of war, or just the fog of growing up. This is why we buy our ticket before getting on the train. We start with the end in mind. But if you've ever purchased a ticket online, you know you also need to know your point of origin. Something I've learned is this: in order to figure out who we are, it's good to know where we've come from. It's wise to invest some time in really getting to know the people who made us, and maybe even the people who made them.

There are any number of ancestry services out there, and I'm not saying they are good or bad. I am saying they aren't enough! If we really want to know ourselves, improve relationships, and enhance our understanding of how to better love others, we should get to know the people who made us. Don't worry, it's OK if no one knows the fourth cousin on your great-great-grandmother's side. That far back might not impact you as much as, say, really knowing who your parents, aunts, uncles, cousins, and grandparents are, and maybe a little about what makes them tick.

As children (and sometimes even as adults), we don't exactly look forward to family reunions or holidays. But that's because we've thought about it as just surviving those few hours before we get back to our own adult life, the inevitable awkward moments, and uncomfortable discussions. What if, instead of just surviving, we considered inquiring? I'm not suggesting a harsh light and interrogation techniques. I think we might be surprised just how much we learn by asking them to tell us what life was like when they were growing up. It can be shocking, in a good and bad way, to hear family talk about the people and events that shaped them.

●   ●   ●

My paternal grandfather, Pop-pop as we called him, had taken over a construction business his father had started. Pop-pop built his own house, and it was filled with so many built-in, semisecret features it was like a spy cave. In his office, he had built a special spring-loaded cabinet to hide the bulky typewriter when not in use. Each closet door had a special mechanism which automatically turned a light in the closet on or off. But I think the coolest invention was in the bathroom: a hidden laundry chute. It opened and dropped down through the floor and into the laundry room on the main level. And much to my grandmother's chagrin,

Pop-pop would even let us kids slide down and plop onto the dirty clothes pile. As luxurious and futuristic as these features seemed to be, Pop-pop was quite the frugal man.

If they say a picture is worth a thousand words, I'm guessing Pop-pop would say a basement is worth $599. When he was building this house, the man in town who owned the bulldozer/backhoe thingamabob (construction knowledge clearly not genetic) wanted $600 to dig a basement. Pop-pop said thank you but no, and promptly grabbed a shovel to dig out his own basement by hand.

Pop-pop had his own look. He wore something like a painter's cap to protect his head from the sun. On the job site he'd frequently have a pencil wedged between the frame of his glasses and the side of his head. It was always the flat kind. (I suppose it fit easier than the round ones we used for school.) His clothes and his car had their own unique smell. Over the years I've flashed back to memories of being next to him in his car or at his shop whenever I am cutting wood and sweating. Some would call it a funk. It's a cross between the sweat of hard work and sawdust. I call it the smell of Pop-pop.

I've been told at times I can be a bit stubborn and have a bit of a one-track mind. I'd say it's my Pop-pop's ability to focus. I realize I've experienced an older, more chilled version of my dad's dad. I'd heard the stories of how Pop-pop would end arguments between my dad and his sister with a single word, one that seems entirely appropriate for a man who could build houses: "Cut!"

●　　●　　●

His son, my dad, was like Pop-pop in his focus, although his focus was athletics. To say my dad grew up as a good athlete would be an understatement. He was a three-sport athletic star even before high school. As a freshman, he earned some playing time as the quarterback on the school's varsity football team. His school honored the athlete of the year; growing up around our house we called this the "Studly Dudly" award. He was the only underclassman to ever be nominated—and he won. I can still recall walks past the high school stadium where he played. He'd recount a certain play, like the time he set the record for the longest touchdown pass. Which, in case you were wondering, still holds today. (At least it did when he was telling me the story.) He wasn't stating it like Bruce Springsteen's "Glory Days," but more to pass on a story about the rewards of hard work mixed with a little luck.

Sadly, he also mentioned how his parents, either by upbringing or perhaps because of their workload, never took much of an interest in his athletic endeavors. In fact, he said his parents rarely attended his games. I always found this odd, considering they lived just across the street, catty-corner from the school. So the great effort both of my parents made to attend my athletic events was not lost on me.

After high school, Dad went on to play at the United States Naval Academy. Then along came this guy you may have heard of, Roger Staubach. Dad gave up pursuing varsity, as it became clear his playing time was going to be limited. He was able to join their one-hundred-fifty-pound team; Dad said it's what they called their JV team. If you ask him today, he'd say, "Oh sure, Roger won the Heisman, played in the NFL, and won a Super Bowl. But I tossed more touchdown passes against Army." And could someone please cue up Bruce? Go Navy, beat Army!

After graduation, Mom and Dad married. Dad wanted to be an astronaut, but to do so he first had to be a pilot. They moved to Florida for flight school. Dad was progressing until one day during routine island hop training, a friend of his, also in training, crashed and was killed. Dad still doesn't talk about it much. Soon after the accident he'd packed up his dreams of flying, being in outer space, and was back at the academy in Maryland. That's where I was born. When he was done with his service requirement, we all moved back to Quakertown for Dad to join the family business. His story of trying to work in his father's construction business revealed two things. My father had little inclination to follow in his father's footsteps, and at the same time showed the unending patience and love of a father. Like Jacob and Isaac. Like God and Jesus ... like we want our earthly father to treat us.

●　　●　　●

They had been working on a church remodel and the plans called for a special-order window to be made. It took a long time for this window to be milled and created because of its unique shape and design. Much of the building had been completed; they had even moved on to other jobs. But after waiting and waiting, the window was delivered to the shop one Saturday morning. Pop-pop asked my dad to deliver and install the window because this would finish up the job.

We've all experienced those moments of self-doubt. Am I up to the task? Even Moses said, "Hey, God, you got the wrong guy, I'm not a good speaker." After the loss of his friend and having given up his dreams of flying in outer space, I think it would be understandable to say my dad maybe had some doubts. Still, with great care, he set about the task from his father.

My Pop-pop had a saying, "You gotta have the right tool for the job." So I'm sure Dad carefully loaded all the necessary tools, ladder, and the window into the back of the Lewis Brothers construction truck. I can imagine him slowly rolling along the roads, maybe even causing a backup like a casual Sunday afternoon driver. He eventually arrived at the jobsite. He carefully set about his task and unloaded all the tools he'd possibly need.

After positioning the ladder and arranging everything, he carefully unloaded the long-awaited, special-order window. The placement of the window was high off the ground, accessible only with the ladder. Can you imagine this? Your job, from your father, is to take a fragile, special-order window for a church, climb up a ladder with the window in hand, and secure it in place. What could possibly go wrong? Having first removed the plywood covering the opening, he carried up the window and started to work its odd shape into its space. He struggled at first, but managed to get it in place. Well, at least part of it. However, when he attempted to correct the alignment, the window moved ever so slightly and was not snugly in place. The ballet of safely staying atop the ladder and properly positioning the window—all while not dropping the window or falling off to his death—must have been grueling. My calves hurt just thinking about it. Each time Dad felt like he had it in place, another side of the window would move. Finally, my dad thought, Maybe if I take my hammer and tap this corner into place, it will stay put and I can get the heck out of here!

Well, we know what happened next. Despite taking extreme care and barely tapping the wood frame, the window cracked.

•　　•　　•

What was that moment like? Maybe you know. Maybe you tried everything you could to save your marriage and still it failed. Maybe you were trying to provide the best care for your child, but they still veered off course, and you wonder if you will ever hear from them, see them, or hold them again. There is good news: God's love is still the right tool for the job. Sometimes we peer into our toolbox of resources, and it is the only tool left.

Maybe we are low on patience or money, or whatever else it is we think we need. Maybe we've lost our faith, our hope, our way, and that's OK. Because the greatest of these is love. His love sits ready at a moment's notice to be liberally dispensed and applied. Use it like those instructions on a shampoo bottle. Wash, rinse, and repeat. My Pop-pop sure did.

Dad set about taking down the broken window, re-covering the hole, loading up the truck, and making the long drive back to the shop. My dad had to go tell his dad what happened. Rather than explode or get angry (which, by the way, is exactly what I would've done), Dad says Pop-pop just looked at him and said, "Well, we'll have to order another window." No lecture, no sigh of disgust, no angry outburst. Dad says it's just who Pop-pop was. He never got mad. I've got my own hand up: I'd like to be more like that.

I'm not saying my grandfather was perfect or God, but in some ways isn't this exactly how our heavenly Father loves us? He sees our strengths and weaknesses. He created us and He knows what we think we are good at doing and all the stuff we'd say, "Ehhhhh, not so much." It's because He knows us better than we know ourselves. He's not afraid, and I daresay takes delight in using the things we wouldn't call our strengths. It's not at all uncommon for Him to take a wrecked marriage, a failed business, the passing of a child, or even something as simple as a broken special-order window to plant the seed that will teach us something.

The window was reordered, eventually came in, and when it did, my dad had to be at least a little worried he'd be asked to go install it. Pop-pop must have known and gently said, "I've got it." Maybe it's time to quiet the voices yelling for our immediate attention. We can be brave in the face of surrendered dreams and repeated failures. And with the love of our heavenly Father, we can begin again each time we've disappointed our dad.

●　　●　　●

My dad telling me the story of the broken window was nothing compared to the story about the day he made his father cry. It was when he told him he was going to marry a Catholic woman. Dad had been raised in a Lutheran home and this announcement had upset his father. Can you imagine that? You were a small-town sports hero. You'd played at one of the nation's military academies and what made your father cry was whom you were choosing to love and spend the rest of your life with. I found myself advocating for my dad. Was this the same Pop-pop who rarely showed up at his games? Was this the same Pop-pop who didn't blow a gasket when Dad shattered the custom window? Was this the same Pop-pop who had provided money for my father and his Catholic wife to leave the family business, move seven hours away, and start some newfangled burger joint?

It was, and soon we headed south to Roanoke, Virginia, a town already familiar with trains, conductors, the fog from steam engines, and being led in different directions. Like the light beaming from the front of a train, Jesus's voice cuts through the fog of our human confusion. Be still, listen, and know the voice. Just like the rhythmic sounds of a train on the rails, Jesus is repeating to us the same message He gave twelve would-be disciples. Two simple words launched the journey for a tax collector, a politician, a thief, and a band of fishermen. The fishermen literally dropped their nets and left their families on the shore.

Have you ever had someone speak to you this way? Was there ever a voice you trusted this much? Maybe the closest thing we can experience comes in the form of those loving words from your pop-pop or dad. But by all accounts, this speaker was a stranger, a nobody—and still they followed.

Centuries later the invitation in the words spoken by the son of a carpenter still stand. They called out to my Pop-pop on each job site. They were whispered to my dad on each rung of the ladder and each step of his journey. And they remain, for you and me. It does not matter what has happened in your past. He doesn't care about the number of mistakes or career tracks you have journeyed down. He's not worried about which version of your life plan you've previously pursued. He just wants to know us and love us. He's still inviting us each day with the same two simple words, "Follow me."

CHAPTER 2

She's A Mother

How do they always seem to know? Maybe, like me, you had a mom who wasn't afraid to squint or raise an eyebrow at your explanations. Maybe more than one time, she intervened just as you were starting trouble, or worse, she showed up at the very end, catching you in the act. Moms seem to have a gift and they call it mother's intuition. I was fortunate to have some good female role models in my life who, like the rest of us, did the best they could.

First and foremost, my mom. She went to school to be a teacher. She also learned many things from the school of hard knocks and taught us kids from this experience. It was partly her idea for my parents to get into the restaurant business. She'd taken a summer job at the local ice cream shop and this experience got her wheels turning. When dad decided life at Lewis Brothers Construction wasn't for him, the restaurant idea surfaced and was pursued.

When we think about it, we all have "other" moms too. In addition to my actual mom, there were many teachers, moms of best friends, and a certain athletic director we all called Momma Duck. Each of these moms supported the work our real moms were doing. They all tried to keep us on the straight and narrow.

The experts say grown-ups tend to change and mellow as they grow from being a new parent to one with experience. Based upon my parents' and my own experience, I would say this is true. I was nervous as a new dad, afraid I'd somehow break my child. I know I was far from perfect but as my child got older, I, too, tended to dial it back. The parenting my youngest two sisters received was vastly different than how the first three children were raised. But perhaps there is no greater change in a person than when they move from parent to grandparent. I'm not a grandpa yet, but I've watched this in my own parents. As they became grandparents themselves, my parents mellowed even more. So let's acknowledge up front the people we experienced as grandmothers were likely very different from the mothers our parents knew.

● ● ●

Babci ("Bob-chi") was my mom's mom. She'd married Dadzi (Polish for grandfather, pronounced, "Ja-gee"—though his friends knew him as Frankie). While he was a public schoolteacher with a side gig of farming and growing plants for landscaping, Babci worked as a seamstress, sang in church and at weddings. I recall sitting next to her in church, her finger would point out the next note and word in the hymnal. And if I sang along, I knew at the end, she'd give me the smile of a proud grandmother.

She loved to cook, sew, and make music. The problem was her cooking often featured cabbage. A ga-wump-ki is literally beef blanketed in cabbage and steamed. Even now, my taste-buds cringe! Lucky for us kids her homemade blankets were made with her love too. She was also handy at fixing the holes we'd inevitably wear into our jeans. But above all else, she loved to sing.

She grew up in the Big Band era and could tell you all the names of all the singers. Crosby, Bennett, Sinatra, the Boswell and Andrew sisters. If there was something she loved more than singing herself, it would be hearing her grandchildren sing. She was at every talent show. She would say things like, "If you are going to sing, sing out, so you can be heard" and "Singing is praying twice!" But she also said, "Don't make shame for the family." We couldn't tell if this was a comment about our singing or behavior.

Every summer, we kids would get two weeks of vacation back in Quakertown, Pennsylvania—one week with Mom's parents and one week with Dad's. Back then we saw it as a great adventure. Now, as an adult, we know what they were doing. No joke, three kids could be a handful for the most talented parent or grandparent. I don't know if we were any more a handful than other kids, but clearly enough our parents needed a two-week reprieve. And our grandparents could survive just a single week each.

The week at my mom's parents was full of playing in the backyard, on the swing set, and wandering through the cornfield. This was decades before the book and movie Children of the Corn, so I truly didn't know any better. Dadzi would stay busy with his landscaping plants and the growing vegetables. I suppose he was indirectly keeping an eye on us as we played. Babci made sandwiches and treats for us in their small kitchen. It was the first room you entered from the back of the house. Each night we had a yummy dinner, treats, and prayers right before bed.

The next week was at Pop-pop and Grammy's. They had a piano and an electronic organ in part because Grammy played for the church choir. Pop-pop would be gone early in the mornings, and I think Grammy wanted us to sleep as long as possible. Still, we would be up and active from the word go. In an attempt to burn off our energy, she would walk us to the school playground, allowing us to climb the ladder for a blistering ride down the hot metal slide. She'd let us swing or spin on the fabric seats of the chain-linked swings and climb the monkey bars to make animal noises.

She was a fighter, a survivor—she'd had breast cancer, open-heart surgery, and diabetes. Her sandwiches were different from Babci's, but still yummy. In the afternoon we'd sit in the shade of their side porch. There we would blow bubbles while we watched and listened to the marching band at the high school as they spent the summer learning music and new marching formations for the upcoming football season. As if this wasn't enough activity, we'd then walk inside: poor Grammy endured our imitation of the marching band as we paraded through the circle of the main floor of her house. From the kitchen to laundry room, through the living and dining areas, finally back into the kitchen, we'd beat pots with wooden spoons and smash lids together to mimic the sights and sounds we'd just watched.

Pop-pop would come home well past five o'clock. Sometimes he fell asleep in his living room chair. Other times he'd pretend to be asleep. Or we'd go to see him and rather than get upset or angry, he'd pretend to be the tickle monster. Oh, how the giggles would fill the house!

But what I saw there was a man busting his butt to make ends meet. His backbone was his wife. She worked in the high school cafeteria during the school year and also worked doing the back-office work for his construction business. And this was just normal.

After dinner, Pop-pop would go to sleep, and Grammy would take us for a walk. We'd hit the sidewalks and look both ways when we had to cross the street. We would walk behind the high school and go straight to where the wild blackberries grew. I am sure it was only a few minutes, but it sure seemed like hours as we would forage for the big ones. Like bears preparing for hibernation, it seemed we ate our weight in those berries.

● ● ●

As we get older, we physically change, we mature emotionally, psychologically, and if we are lucky, spiritually. Likewise, the relationship with both my grandmothers also changed. Of course, it was a big thrill for me to grow taller than they were. But our relationship would also see other heights. I remember driving each of them for the first time. I am sure they were as nervous as my parents but said nothing but positive things. I can recall attending church services with each of them. While they each celebrated God in a different denomination, they shared more in common than not. Each was proud of the unique things that made up her church. As I got older, they both tried to ask questions about my sports and who I was dating. They were there cheering me on until the end.

Grammy was the first to die. I was living in Nashville and had randomly received a letter from her. It was months past my birthday and nowhere close to Christmas. She wrote to tell me she was in the hospital again as doctors did some routine monitoring of her heart. She shared her plans to come for a visit as she and Pop-pop would head south to Florida for the winter. She never made the trip. She died about a week after I received the letter. I later learned my sisters and other family members had also received a similar letter, and this let me know that maybe she knew.

I watched Babci pick up and carry on after Dadzi had passed from the effects of a lifetime of smoking and drinking. For years she'd continued to pick us up for visits to her house on Friday nights, but as she aged, this all changed. She struggled to keep up her home and eventually agreed to move into assisted living.

She fell and broke her hip. I recall visiting her, but by then the dementia had scrambled her mind. Our visits consisted of four or five conversations repeating as if on a loop. And yet the mind is a mystery. The night she passed away, we gathered around and sang the old Polish songs she'd taught us. While she struggled to give voice, the twinkle in her eye let us know she knew the words. We watched as the priest came and gave final blessings. We were there as the last breath left her lungs. When it was time to go home, I stopped at the restaurant she'd always taken us to on Friday nights. It seemed entirely appropriate.

The women, the grandmothers, and other mothers play a unique role critical to each stage of our growing up. It doesn't matter where we live, the women in our lives play a crucial role.

●　　●　　●

I grew up on Chestnut Mountain, a neighborhood in the eastern edge of Roanoke County, Virginia. It's a valley tucked into the foothills of the Blue Ridge Mountains. It's not uncommon for storm clouds to hug the mountains as they enter or exit the valley.

Like most kids, I thought summers were the best. All the neighborhood kids would stay out late playing games like basketball, kickball, and kick-the-can. When it was time to come home, my mother would step out on the porch and call for us. We knew that voice. Each kid in the neighborhood knew the distinctive call of his mom. When you heard your call, even if it was your turn, you dropped everything and headed for home. We knew if they had to call a second time, we'd better be running home. We knew who our master was, and we knew our master's voice. That was the shepherd's voice of our day. In gospel times, shepherds tended their flocks in a common pasture with sheep of different flocks intermingled, not unlike us kids growing up on the mountain.

Have you ever wondered what Jesus's mom was like? I wonder if she ever stepped outside and yelled His name? Did Jesus ignore her or start home like we did? We know her name was Mary. We know she was very young when the angel Gabriel visited her. We can read her honest questions and her humble accepting response. We see her holding her baby, our Savior, there in the manger. We assume there were many loving, nurturing moments from the manger to the moment she found Him teaching in the synagogue. But the same void from Jesus' first preaching in the synagogue to the beginning of His ministry is also missing in Mary's story.

Maybe, like me, you've genuinely wondered—did Mary spank Jesus? How many time-outs did Jesus earn in a day? And finally, did Jesus do His chores and eat everything His mother put on His plate? We can laugh about these things, but one thing is clear: Jesus' relationship with His mother was also very special. Unlike Joseph, we do see Mary again. She's there for Jesus' ministry and there at the very end. And as painful as it was to lose my grandmothers, as hard as it can be when our mothers pass away, imagine the pain and reversal Mary felt when she was there with Jesus at the cross. Maybe you don't have to imagine what it is like to watch your child die. We think our moms are supposed to make our boo-boos all better, not bury their children. I think this is just another reason why it's fair to say there is something for us to learn from our mothers, especially Jesus' mother, Mary.

There is a song popular around Christmastime that asks the question, "Mary, did you know?" Like my Grammy knew, I think Mary probably also knew there was something about her Son. I mean, after all, an angel appeared to let her know she would become a mother. Like my Babci, I think she likely wasn't clear on every detail or the full extent of just how special her Son would be. But like the good mothers, she did know when it was time for Him to start. Turning water into wine would prove to be far more than a neat wedding trick. It was the beginning of Jesus' ministry here on earth.

Are you sitting with your aging mother right now? Has she already passed, and you miss her more every day? Or are you a mother, sitting and listening to your child's doctor say they've done all they can? Are you the child whose mother beat them, left them, or gave them up for adoption? What miracle, what answer, are you seeking? Like us, I am sure Mary had many questions on the journey from Bethlehem to Golgotha; some she was able to ask and get answers from her Son. As Mary did with Jesus, we have to be humble enough and wise enough to ask our mothers to share their wisdom. When it's not possible, we can direct our questions upward. But even then, we may not get the obvious burning bush answer. The point is God welcomes our questions. We know this because He said to inherit heaven we had to be more like the children.

I had a cousin who, when he was younger, asked a lot of questions. So much so that his mom and teachers treated him like a baseball player—instead of a pitch count, he was limited to a certain number of questions every class period. Once he exceeded his limit, the adults told him to "save it." Thankfully, God doesn't work like that. If anything, He says "bring it."

"Look to the LORD and his strength; *seek* his face always."

"Now devote your heart and soul to *seeking* the LORD your God."

"God did this so that they would *seek* him and perhaps reach out to him and find him, though he is not far from any one of us."

"You will *seek* me and find me when you *seek* me with all your heart."

"But *seek* first his kingdom and his righteousness, and all these things will be given to you as well."

"I love those who love me, and those who *seek* me find me."

"For you LORD, have never forsaken those who *seek* you."

"So I say to you: Ask and it will be given to you; *seek* and you will find; knock and the door will be opened to you. For everyone who asks receives; the one who *seeks* finds; and to the one who knocks, the door will be opened."

God isn't afraid of our questions; in fact, He welcomes them. He already knows about your parents, grandparents, and the rest of your family tree. He knows about all of their stuff and how that stuff contributed to your stuff. What God wants more than anything is a relationship with each of us. He wants us to be pressing in, asking, seeking, and knocking on the doors of heaven as we attempt to make sense of it all.

And here's a little secret: it will never make 100 percent sense in the moment. If we are lucky we will look back years later and see where a particular event prompted a change in us. There's a song about unanswered prayers you may have heard. And its message is true. Life has taught us sometimes the answer we need, is not the one we hoped for. Often the outcome varies from what we plan. We aren't disqualified from God if our relationships with moms and grandmothers aren't perfect. We can trust that even if He seems silent, our heavenly Father is leaning ever closer, telling us to press in with our questions and pursuit of Him.

CHAPTER 3

A Smaller World

I remember our first house in Vinton, Virginia. Have you ever had the experience of going back to your childhood home after some years and everything seems so small? When you were a kid it was big—it was your entire universe—but now it's just somebody's starter home. That's the feeling I get whenever I slowly turn around in the cul-de-sac and see the house on Abbey Circle. One of my first memories there was learning to write my name. K-E-V-I-N, five letters that, in my brain, were easier to write in capital letters. Maybe because they were just a bunch of connected straight lines. I still didn't quite understand the concept of upper- or lowercase letters or even why it was important.

I knew I had a middle name, but this part was confusing for me. There was rarely a mention of my dad's middle name. In all the stories of his athletics, everyone called him Bobby. But the legend of his athleticism did not seem to fit the only other kid I knew with the name—Bobby Brady. If building your personal brand had existed back then, I'm sure my dad would have been billed as the Amazing Bobby Lewis. But now he was my dad, and everyone just called him Bob. They said it was short for Robert and this was the confusing part for me. Wouldn't a shortened version of Robert be Rob? At least I knew why we all had the same last name. But this day I was intently focused on writing my first name. Maybe that's when the journey to self began. Regardless, this day I had a blue crayon in my hand.

The house we lived in was a split-level. The left-hand side went upstairs, and the right side led to the lower level. There I was, on the bottom step leading to the upstairs. It was just me and a blue crayon. I remember looking around and seeing the wall. It was above the stair I was sitting on but not above the rise of the next. The small pocket of space looked like paper and so I began writing the K on the wall. I had to be around five years old, and I can't remember if I used my right or left hand. It wasn't looking pretty but it was definitively a K. I moved on to the E and the next letter and got all the way to the end. That's when Mom showed up.

I don't know if she was going downstairs, coming up from the lower level, or just magically appearing, as moms tend to do when they sense something is up. At first, I thought, Mom's gonna be so proud and happy with her only boy. I just knew she'd be thrilled I'd learned to write when she saw what I'd done.

Instead, it was the first time I would feel the weight of hearing my first, middle, and last name. She added, "Wait until your father gets home!" I don't think I was spanked but I knew she wasn't happy. I don't recall if I was sent to my room or if I just ran there. I climbed in my bed to self-soothe, process the event, or, like most five-year-olds, probably just to sulk. I do remember Dad coming home but can't remember his reaction beyond an initial snicker and then a serious face. I just remember Mom washing the wall afterwards.

Now I know this may seem like a not-so-big deal. A normal kid thing, followed by a normal mom reaction, followed by cleaning it all up. But in the moment to this five-year-old, it was the first time I remember feeling ashamed of my name. It's taken nearly a half century for the person I am now to convince five-year-old me it was OK. And still there are days when the five-year-old looks back and asks, "Are you sure?" As an adult, I get it. But for a little kid, it was hard to figure out why Mom didn't share my joy. I'm not blaming my mother. She is a good mom and an adoring grandmother.

•　　•　　•

Mom wouldn't describe herself as the daughter of a man who drank a lot. She didn't need to. We knew. It explained why her father never wanted us near his liquor bottle collection in the basement at his house and the PBR we watched him drink. It explained "Happy Frankie"—those times when he was overly friendly and goofy. I suppose he was trying his best too.

Mom also told us how her mom used to threaten to "biff" her upside the head. Sometimes with just her bare hand and other times while wielding a frying pan. In my mind, the image stood in stark contrast to the grandparents I had come to know. Surely, Mom couldn't have meant the same hand that showed me how to sing.

It wasn't always this confusing. There were just three of us to begin with. My older sister was nearly four years older than me. My younger sister was just sixteen months behind me. We had hand-me-down furniture, still usable and nice. I remember one big chair and how when the seat cushions were adjusted just right, it became the front end and windshield portions of a car. The back cushion would be fixed above and instantly I was in a convertible Corvette or dune buggy, whichever I felt like driving that day. The car provided great escapes when we needed them.

Along with driving furniture, I would escape outside to learn how to ride my bike in the driveway. It had a gentle slope to it. I remember not wanting to have training wheels and convincing

Dad I had enough balance to remove the wheels on one side. He must've thought it was a good idea because I can remember leaning hard to one side whenever I needed stability. Eventually the second wheel came off. Now this wasn't the fancy banana seat with the tricked-out handlebars, mind you, just an ordinary, blue, hand-me-down bike. I would walk it up the slight incline of our driveway connecting to the cul-de-sac. I turned the bike around and glanced at what looked like a runway's length. After a deep breath of courage I'd manage to push off and coast down the gentle slope toward our house.

Remember how small things seemed bigger then? Well, that must've been the case with our driveway. I thought I had plenty of time to get my balance before having to pedal backwards to apply the brake, but I was wrong. I quickly found myself driving the front wheel into the brick chimney at the base of the driveway. It would've been fine if that was it, but I was learning what it was like to be airborne and going over the handlebars. I can't remember what part of my body hit the chimney first. Maybe it was my head, but there was no blood. I was startled but not broken. Just like we do for most of our lives, I got back up and tried again.

I was glad none of the neighbor girls saw that. The Bruckmans lived next door—Debbie, Pam, and Collette. Each of them at one time or another was our babysitter. Suffice it to say they earned whatever amount my parents paid them. But occasionally, there was an adventure that became a memory, like the time Pam made Jiffy Pop popcorn.

●　　●　　●

I don't know what was so magical about a pie tin full of popcorn seeds with a little handle. Maybe it's the cool way they twist-fold the foil covering the kernels. Maybe it's the way the foil appears to magically unfold and get larger with each pop. But we knew it was special when the Jiffy Pop came out.

Pam started the popcorn and at some point, must've helped herself to a jar of pickles. Maybe we distracted her. It's not hard to imagine our noise level beckoned her out of the kitchen, away from the stove. I recall we were all downstairs on the lowest level. I know at some point her hand got caught in the pickle jar. One moment we were laughing and thinking she was faking her captivated hand. The next moment the upstairs smoke detector/fire alarm was blaring.

We'd had fire drills in school, but this was the real deal. Now keep in mind this was before cell phones and 911. But we did at least have phones, although with all the smoke in the kitchen you might have thought we were sending smoke signals. Pam did the smart thing and tossed our beloved Jiffy Pop outside, thus removing the source of smoke. But she had no idea how to turn off the smoke detector. With the screech and beeping of the alarm it was not hard for me to start living out scenes from my favorite television show.

I could hear the communications chatter: "Emergency! Rampart, Rampart, we have a single-alarm Jiffy Pop fire in progress." While I prepared to meet John Gage and Roy DeSoto, I secretly hoped they would have to transport me to Rampart and into the care of Dr. Kelly Brackett—and especially nurse Dixie McCall.

Meanwhile back in the real world of our kitchen, Pam was trying to dial the phone, one hand holding the phone and the other in a pickle jar making attempts to punch in the touch-tone number to her mom's house next door. My oldest sister jumped in and helped dial the number. Soon, the familiar face of Mrs. B was at our house. We exited to the front porch while she opened the windows to begin airing out the house. Eventually the alarm turned off and we had a story to tell for the ages.

● ● ●

How easy is it for us to get caught with our hands in the pickle jar? Burning popcorn, screeching smoke detectors, and screaming kids aside—wait, hold on. On second thought, don't put them to the side but maybe call them something else. How many times have you been so self-determined to see a situation end with your resolution? I will guarantee Pam had no plans to burn the popcorn and set off the smoke detector. She made an honest mistake and got distracted. So much so, even her attempts to call for help were hampered by a hand caught in a pickle jar. So I'll ask again: How many times has each of us been so distracted and yet self-determined to see a situation end with a specific resolution?

Maybe it was a job interview or an actual first job. Maybe it was your first middle school puppy love crush, a first marriage (your second or third). Maybe it was the time you had an argument and said things you really didn't mean. You planned to apologize but the next day turned into weeks, then years, and then the person passed away. The point is to not beat ourselves up.

In the Bible, our relationship with God is described in many ways. One of the names He has is Father. I know for some, their experience with their father is great. And yet there are many who would speak of their experience as not so good—or even nonexistent. If you've experienced the latter, here's a chance to start again with a heavenly Father. Speaking as someone who has messed things up more than once, let me say it's worth the risk. There is another image of our relationship with the Creator—that of shepherd and sheep.

When I first heard of this relationship I didn't know much about herding or animals. All I could grasp was I was the sheep. At first this seemed like the baaaaaaaaaad end of the deal. (Almost as bad as that joke.) But perhaps my joke makes the point. He is the Good Shepherd, and we are the sheep for a reason. It's not to say we are completely stupid and mindless, walking around making noises and looking for our next meal. (Although, despite our decisions sometimes we, like the Israelites, end up doing exactly that.) What separates us from everything else in creation is this: we were created in His image. Our Father gives us free will. We can wander here and there, or wonder about this or that. Yes, on more than one occasion we've been, and will be, the sheep who wander off.

Maybe you have spent far too much time trying to make something happen. Perhaps it's not meant to be or maybe it's not meant to be right now. Maybe it's something darker. Maybe the something has isolated you from friends, your job, your family. Have you ever found yourself in a very dark place? The only thing worse than being there is trying to find your way back from that place.

The employer, the friends, and maybe even the family relationships you burned along the way ... they seem to want to have nothing to do with you. Maybe it's even harder. Maybe they feel justified because of your actions, or they think they are doing the right thing and showing you some tough love. I don't know the specifics of what you are facing, but if we've spent any time at all on this earth, we've all been there! Thankfully, He is the Good Shepherd for a reason. He does know the situation. He knows what you've done and where you are. And still He searches for you!

There's a story about a shepherd with one hundred sheep. One of them wandered off. In the story, he leaves the ninety-nine to go searching for the one. Maybe, like me, you don't know much about herding. Still, even we know leaving ninety-nine for one seems like a really big risk. For starters, just the math of it. What's the plan for the ninety-nine? I can't imagine this shepherd had all the modern tools or fencing required to build a pen safe enough to protect ninety-nine sheep. I know there are things like poachers or predators who would see ninety-nine sheep and prepare for a feast. If I were the shepherd, I would certainly think twice about leaving ninety-nine for one.

But this is not the case with the Good Shepherd in this story. He is the heavenly Father I mentioned earlier. He doesn't think twice. He sees us as more than worth any risk to the other ninety-nine. Perhaps calling out to Him would not be a baaaaaaaaad place to start. And that's no joke.

It might seem pointless. It might seem like He's not coming to help you. Others you've hurt or even the voices from within will try to convince you: "You're not worth it." Or "After all you've done, you deserve this." Don't believe them! Even if it takes a while, the Shepherd has already started His search. He's on his way, slowly, methodically; He is coming and will find you.

Perhaps it's just time for you to sit with your blue crayon, be still with your popcorn or jar of pickles and know this. The rescue mission is underway. Wait, listen—you will hear the Shepherd's voice. Do not be afraid of what will happen when He finds you. I can tell you, in the story (and my own experience), He will pick you up, place you on His shoulders, and carry you back. Let Him.

CHAPTER 4

Closer to the Truth

As a kid, they tell you to never look at the sun during the day. It could burn your eyeballs out! While it never did burn mine out, it would leave the annoying dot in my vision for hours. But at this time of day, it was apparently OK to take in the beauty of an evening sunset. I could see the sun getting lower in the sky and I must've stopped building the next great highway with my Tonka bulldozer and dump truck. Sitting there in the sand box, just watching the sun, still burning in all of its bright orange and red hues, I was transfixed watching it from my small, square beach.

A familiar voice disrupted the moment. It was my mom calling my name. I looked around but didn't see her. Maybe I was imagining it. But there it was again. Mom was inside preparing dinner for her small army. She must've called to me through the open kitchen window. Our little split-level was very nice but by no means a mansion. I had exited the downstairs to access the backyard and my sandbox. Our kitchen was also on the back side of the house and the kitchen window overlooked the backyard and a tall tree. Turns out Mom hadn't seen me, she just called out thinking I was inside the house. But she probably could see me if I were in that tree, I thought. If there's one thing I enjoyed more than my Tonkas, it was climbing trees. Mainly because at this age I thought I could grow up to be a monkey, climb trees, and eat bananas all day. Oh, the dreams of a child.

I started to work my way up the tree as I continued to hear Mom call my name. At this point I wasn't ignoring her, just attempting to position myself to better see and communicate with her. The tree I was climbing rose just above the roof of our house. I knew better than to climb too high, but I also knew I could still get up and be just as high as the kitchen window. I had made this climb several times before. The tree was not right next to the house but maybe twenty feet from the window. As I reached my perch, I could see in the window and, indeed, Mom was cooking something in the kitchen. She called my name again and this time I replied with a loud, "What?"

She answered, "Come here, I need you."

I said, "Mom, I'm right here."

She turned around as if looking for something or someone. I wasn't there so she called my name again. I truly wasn't trying to hide or torment her when I replied again, "I'm right here."

This time she turned and walked away from the window. I could still hear her calling my name and asking, "Exactly where is here?"

It occurred to me she thought I was playing a game of hide and seek, so I couldn't help but start to laugh. She eventually reappeared at the window, perhaps surmising it was the last location she had heard my voice. She called out once more, but this time adding my middle name. It doesn't take a genius to realize a mom is losing her patience when she starts adding your middle name. The gig was up, but I couldn't stop giggling. I said, "Mom, I'm right here. Look outside the window."

Her eyes looked up as she leaned closer to the open window. She looked to her left, then down, and then to her right. Our eyes met and her chin dropped. In an instant, she had gone from increasing frustration to genuine concern. Equally as fast, she managed to appear out the back door. Again, using my first, middle, and last name. I thought, Oh great, I'm in trouble again.

I was taking my time carefully getting down the tree, half trying to demonstrate my climbing prowess and half hoping to delay what I thought for sure was another spanking. Eventually, I made it all the way down and then the unexpected occurred. Instead of a spanking, my mom wrapped her arms around me and hugged me. She wasn't mad at all! She had been scared to see me so high and was glad her little "sonny boy" was alive. It's the surprise ending that sticks with me and reminds me of the turning point in the story of Zacchaeus.

● ● ●

In the Bible, Zacchaeus was a tax collector. He got rich by cheating people. He kept a portion of their tax for himself. You can probably imagine ol' Zach wasn't super popular with the people in town. Zacchaeus had heard Jesus was coming to town and he was determined to lay eyes on the guy everyone seemed to be talking about. Zach was a short guy and didn't stand much of a chance of seeing anything amongst the crowd. Then he thought of an idea.

He climbed a tree. From there he figured he could easily keep an eye on the road and see when Jesus was coming. The crowds grew bigger and soon Jesus was walking down the road. Imagine the scene up there in the tree branch: a long road, but off in the distance you see even more people gathering and surrounding this one guy. There are a thousand and one images of how "they" say Jesus looked. Plug in the image you have in your mind. Now imagine seeing His face from far off getting closer and closer to where you are.

When I was growing up, the images I saw on TV were music stars. Groups like the Beatles, the Rolling Stones, and Elvis would make appearances, and throngs of fans showed up, yelling and screaming their names. Can you see it? Maybe you've been to a concert for your favorite singer or group. Can you feel it? The fever pitch right before they take the stage. The lights dim and everyone screams. Suddenly there's a small light. It comes on just enough to see the back-lit image of someone scampering on the stage. It could be the lead singer, maybe someone in the band, or perhaps it's just a roadie grabbing something left behind from the opening act. It doesn't matter who it is because everyone is hyped, screaming, and ready. That day in the tree, Zacchaeus was ready.

Now imagine it's you in the tree. The scene is playing out as some guy approaches along the dusty road in the middle of the day. He's walking closer and closer to you in the tree. Suddenly He stops just under your branch. Just like my mom looked and saw me out the window, this rock star rabbi looks straight up and locks eyes with you. As if this weren't enough, He clearly and loudly calls out your name from the stage, I mean the road. "Zacchaeus," says this smiling Jesus, "come, get down from there. I want to hang out and stay at your house today!"

What would you do? Would you believe His words, or quietly question if His request was legit? Zacchaeus climbed down. I imagine it was with a mix of pride and a fair dose of surprise as he said something like "Ummmm … sure, you are welcome to come to my house."

Meanwhile, the others in the crowd, what did they do? They knew who Zacchaeus was and had to be questioning, "Does this Jesus know who He's talking to?" Maybe they even wondered aloud, "Why does Jesus want to go home with him?"

Maybe sensing he was caught in the act, Zacchaeus turned to Jesus and said, "Hey ... I promise to give half of my money to the poor and if I have cheated anyone in taxes, I'll pay them back four times the amount."

How did Jesus respond? How would you respond? I think if I were in the crowd, I'd be hoping to hear Jesus say something like, "Oh, wait a second, you're Zacchaeus? That Zacchaeus? Never mind, I got the wrong guy."

But that's not at all what Jesus said. In fact, He proclaimed, "Salvation comes to Zacchaeus' house today! For I have come to look for and to seek those who are lost."

I had a coach who one day paraphrased something I've since seen in the Bible. Coach would say, "Men let your actions speak so clearly you don't even have the need for words." Since then, it's never lost on me how my actions, what I actually do, are far more important than anything I could ever say.

Jesus' actions matched up with the words He'd already spoken. It was no accident Jesus spotted Zacchaeus in the tree. The act of calling out to him was already forgiveness. Even before he'd made his offer of repayment, Zacchaeus got forgiveness—whether he deserved it or not.

● ● ●

The same thing happened to my dad one time. He'd borrowed a non-Tonka truck to run some errands. The guy said, "Hey, the lights don't work, so be done before dark." We kids were Dad's labor force; perhaps this is why the work took a little longer than expected. Sure enough, heading home we were just about to make the turn in to our subdivision when the flashing lights came on. We were being pulled over.

I was squished in the back of the cab and watched as the officer approached the vehicle. He made eye contact with me before he spoke to my dad. He explained the reason he pulled us over, asking if there was a reason Dad had chosen to not use the vehicle's lights. This is the moment my Superman took off his cape.

Rather than repeat what his friend had told him earlier in the day, Dad responded, "Ummmm, yeah, well, actually, I had thought to put them on, but they flickered on and off and now don't stay on."

I don't know if I made an audible gasp, but I am pretty sure my chin fell wide open. Just like my mom's did when she saw me so high in the tree. Fortunately, the officer stayed focused on his conversation with my dad and didn't look back at me. Dad did mention the truck was borrowed from a friend and also pointed out we'd pulled over in the turnoff to our neighborhood.

The officer did what many good officers do. He assessed the situation and information as presented to him and applied a dose of common sense. He sent my dad on his way.

But as soon as the officer was out of range, I gasped, "Dad, you just lied to a cop!" My grandmother often told us there were certain things you could do to earn a spot on the Hell Express. As a child, it didn't take much to imagine a train complete with flames and demons racing to its downward destination. I think this was her way of scaring good behavior into us. I was just a little kid, but I was fairly sure lying to a police officer was somewhere on the list. Of course, Dad recognized what he'd done; he even said to us it was wrong. But I wonder if Dad's experience wasn't something like what Zacchaeus probably felt.

●　　●　　●

Zacchaeus had become rich by cheating people. But what did Jesus see? He saw someone so excited to see Him he had literally climbed a tree to get a better view. Jesus knew what Zacchaeus had done, He didn't need to hear any story. Still, He smiled at Zacchaeus and said, "Brother, I wanna hang with you!" or something spiritual along those lines.

The day Zacchaeus met Jesus he became a new man. Of course, he'd heard about Jesus's power and love. But on this day, more than hearing about this guy, he actually met Him. Zach experienced both power and love, firsthand. Would you be as brave as Zacchaeus and consider meeting this Jesus guy you'd heard about? Zacchaeus didn't need to use words, but he did. He promised to pay back even more than any amount he'd taken. He got real and knew he had done so many people wrong. He wanted to be forgiven by Jesus. But what about the crowd? They didn't like the sound of this at all. They, too, needed to consider something new, but they didn't even know it.

Why did they—and why do we—need new hearts? Because just like them, we need to forgive, just as Jesus did. Being real in our faith is not a matter of simply loving or believing in Jesus. It's not a matter of simply knowing and following a certain set of rules or perfectly obeying the Ten Commandments. It involves turning from our old ways, the ones that perhaps feel like second nature. They're as ingrained as the tracks of the Tonka bulldozer in my sandbox. They are habits as natural as a mom's reaction to seeing her child high in a tree, and as instinctive as trying to talk our way out of a ticket. The old ways rationalize a little lie here and there. Turning away from the old ways? This is the hard work.

As a kid, my parents always told us when we mess up it's not enough to say we're sorry—we've got to take action and seek to make things right. Sometimes it may not be entirely possible. But this is what it takes when we are trying to live and love as Jesus did. It's not easy, especially when we remove the "stealing money" Zacchaeus did and plug in what we've done or the something someone did to us.

I've seen in the news, instances when the mother of someone who was killed confronts the person who murdered her child with an impact statement. I think I know how I would react, and maybe you do too. I know I am blown away by the moments when the words the mother speaks are nothing but complete love and forgiveness. It can be hard to separate the sin from the sinner. So what can we do? Well, maybe the tax collector can teach us something after all.

Zacchaeus sought out this Jesus. He dared to climb a tree and certainly couldn't have even imagined he would have the opportunity to meet Jesus, personally speak to Him, host Him in his house, and break bread with Him.

Another story in the Bible says "if we seek God, we can find Him." I think it's easy to question where God is when we don't see a clear path out of our circumstance. It's easier to trust the image of the Shepherd finding the sheep who wandered off. But we have something Zacchaeus didn't, a flare gun, of sorts—called prayer. Rather than choosing to remain lost, what would happen if we more readily sent up our flare? These days prayer is our best chance to communicate with God. Let's take the shot.

Seeking Him should be an easy, natural thing to do. So why is it we think we can fix it alone? Why do we busy ourselves like children in a sandbox? We are not alone. God has sent someone to you in those moments. Maybe it's not a burning bush or an angelic cloud. Maybe it's a friend or family member's kind words. Perhaps it's the memory of something a teacher or coach said to you years earlier. Let those voices remind you. You are not alone. Be still and listen.

Maybe our answers aren't as obvious as the officer's flashing lights and siren behind us. I don't really know if my dad ever reached out, apologized to the officer or confessed the whole story. And I'm not just trying to let my dad off the hook. On more than one occasion, he and I disagreed, occasionally even argued. Once we didn't even speak for a few years. But I also know that oftentimes our earthly parents, broken as they may be, do their best to mimic God's love for us. Here's a little secret: no human, no parent, is perfect. Sometimes it looks like a mother scolding her child for climbing a tree but ends up being an embrace, thankful you are safe. At other times we tell a little lie to avoid trouble, and while that's not a good thing, we should consider the entirety of one's actions. For me, I know my parents remained open to new ways of the spirit and lived out actions that, even more than words, pointed me upward.

CHAPTER 5

Little League Life Lessons

I t was awkward and cool at the same time. And it's no surprise a three-sport high school sports star wanted his kids to be involved in sports too. He was my first coach and I remember the first sport I played was T-ball. Who doesn't like the idea of T-ball? Granted, for the seasoned sports fan, taking in a T-ball game may be just slightly more exciting than watching paint dry. But as a first step into athletics, playing it as a kid was perfect.

The ball isn't hurled at you, so no one ever got hit by an errant pitch. Every at bat it was just sitting there atop its perch, motionless and almost floating in the air like a balloon "stands" on its string. You know, when it has lost enough helium so it can't float to the ceiling, but not so much that it's lying on the floor. Now T-ball is much like baseball, but here is where the rules more accurately reflect the American ideal: every kid gets a chance to walk up to the plate and launch the ball over the fence—or right back to the "pitcher's" glove, whichever the case may be. It didn't matter if you were a boy, a girl, black, white, brown, purple, or orange. You had a chance.

All T-ball teams are the same. You have those kids who take it very seriously. They either have overbearing parents or are just very focused on baseball. At the other end of the spectrum are those who find four-leaf clovers or chase butterflies and grasshoppers in the outfield. And of course, there is a wide variety of baseball ability in between those two extremes.

Unfortunately, T-ball also reflects another American reality: some kids had a better shot than others. They were either the coach's kids, older, stronger, bigger, or just plain good at the basics of baseball. Our team had one of those. Even though I was younger, I could tell there was something special about him. I was sure he would play pro ball. After all, even though we were just kids, he had a baseball bag! It carried his cleats, his mitt, and his batting gloves. His bat had its own slot on the side, and there was even a pocket to hold really important stuff like bubble gum or a few coins so he could go to the concession stand all by himself.

Let's call him Brad. And don't get me wrong—Brad wasn't a cocky, I'm-better-than-you kind of kid. But, boy, was he confident. The kind of guy you wanted to hang around. He played first base because he was so good at catching the ball, no matter how errant our throws over to him. He could stretch to the sky, step to the left or right, and darn near do a split that would make the best gymnast appreciate his effort. At least this is how I remember him. If you think Brad was good at first base, you should've seen him hit. Brad batted last, and if you don't remember the nuance of T-ball, this was a huge honor. Every kid got to hit every inning, but when the last batter came up, everyone knew it. The kids in the field backed up and everyone in the stands scooted to the edge of their seats.

There's a scene in the Bible, you know the one, when Jesus made water into wine and it left the guy questioning, "Hey, why did you save the best for last?" While it might not have been the norm to do with wine at a wedding, it was what every team did in T-ball. Being named the last batter was like punching your ticket to Cooperstown. While I didn't exactly know where Cooperstown was or why a baseball player would want to leave our town and move there, all the kids talked about it so I just played along. We dropped Cooperstown into as many sentences as possible. In the fog of our five- to seven-year-old brains, if anyone could make it to that town, it would be Brad.

He would take his bat and do his warm-up swings. He looked just like the guys on TV. When he walked to the plate, he didn't have to drag his bat like most of the kids. If they had T-ball in biblical times, Brad was like Sampson or a good-guy version of the giant. Big, tall, strong, and man, could he do it all.

● ● ●

You know what is really great? God sees all of us just like I remember Brad. God isn't concerned with your batting average or on-base percentage. He isn't impressed if you have the right bag with all the pockets, and He's not ashamed if all you have is a hand-me-down glove and no bat of your own. He is equally proud and excited for the kid who hits it over the fence, as He is for the one picking flowers in the outfield. Or the kid like me, who wanted to slide into every base and developed a disco-like way of shaking his backside to dust off his Toughskins jeans after every attempt. God loves you too. He loves all of us exactly the same. I understood this a little better when I became a parent. God looks at each of us and lovingly proclaims, "That's my child!"

At one of these games I was almost embarrassed to say, "That's my dad." I don't remember who we were playing, and I am not even sure if we won the game. I'm almost afraid to ask my dad these questions.

Do you know those people who can rattle off facts, Bible verses, or random things you didn't know? My dad was one of those when I was growing up—especially about sports. He would likely play it off these days, but back then he was the walking, talking version of a sports encyclopedia, a virtual Siri for sports information. His memory for the rules of the game, and specific plays is impressive. When we watched football on TV he even taught me to watch the offensive line. If they fired forward it was a run play. If they stood straight up or stepped backwards it was a pass. But this day there was the Play. The play at the plate. Well, at least that's where it started.

Our team was on defense; we already had the first two outs and needed just one more to end the inning. The "two away" chatter arose and I echoed as if I fully understood what it meant. I imagine there was one of those big movie scenes where the pitcher looked in for the catcher's signal, maybe he even shook off the sign once or twice. But this was just T-ball, no actual pitching. The game was played at Vinton's War Memorial Field.

The other team's version of "Brad" was at the plate. There was a crack of the bat and the ball was hit hard to the outfield. The opposing team's runners advanced and some were crossing the plate. The ball was relayed and there would be a tight play at the plate. The runner came charging down the third baseline. Our catcher, Todd, caught the throw, glanced, and prepared for the impending collision. There was a huge cloud of dust as the two players met. Then a cheer from the opposing team and their fans, as it appeared the play went their way. Their player got up and went to celebrate the play with his third base coach and teammates. Todd and the rest of us got ready for the next play. And this is when my dad came out of our dugout.

I'd like to insert again that he was our coach and not the crazy stereotypical sports dad who came out of the stands and onto the field. This little fact seemed to make me feel better in the moment.

My teammates saw our coach, but to me, it was my dad. He was emphatic about something, but I, my teammates, and pretty much everyone else seemed to have no idea what he was talking about.

I watched as Dad talked, walking with our catcher in tow. Together they went down the third baseline and headed straight for the other team's dugout. Now at this point I had very little life experience, let alone game experience. All I knew was this wasn't like any other game we'd played before. There was never a play in our league or on TV where a manager and player walked over to the other team's dugout. In my little-kid brain, this wasn't looking good. It looked to me like Dad was starting a fight, and I imagined the whole team being arrested and hauled off to jail. There was even a little confrontation at the entrance to the other team's dugout. Their manager stood by the entrance. My dad said something to Todd and he looked back at my dad as if to say, "What?" The other team's manager started hollering, saying, "He can't come in here!" while attempting to block Todd.

By this time even the umpire had worked his way to the scene. I heard my dad saying, "Todd, you take the ball, walk in there, and tag him out." With the other team's manager still protesting, Todd's face now looked as though my dad had just told him to walk into a lion's den. But to Todd's credit, he did what was asked. He walked past the manager, the other players, and found the kid he'd just finished colliding with moments earlier. He applied the tag and the umpire shouted, "He's out!" You can probably imagine how the scene played out. The other team, their manager, and their fans could not believe what had just unfolded. But my dad and the umpire knew something no one else in the crowd did.

During the play at the plate, the kid never touched home base. The umpire never gave a call and my dad saw this. He knew what it meant. The play was not over. Had Dad not been paying close attention and we'd moved forward with the next batter, the play and the run would've counted. But he didn't miss it. He was paying attention and we got the out. Now this was one play in one game.

I'm not even sure we won. It didn't advance us to the playoffs, and we sure didn't make the T-ball World Series that year. But in the moment, it was a big deal.

● ● ●

How many signs, how many answers to prayer, how many affirmations do we miss simply because we weren't paying attention? Jesus knew what it was like for His audience to not get it. We aren't talking about a ragtag group of T-ballers, we are talking about the disciples. I don't know about you, but more often than not I see the disciples portrayed as the first inner circle, the group of Holy Rollers who have it all together, right? Wrong! One of them wrote about a time when Jesus had been preaching to the same crowd for a number of days. It came time for everyone to leave but Jesus didn't want them to leave on a long journey without food. The disciples had just seven loaves of bread and some fish. Of course, Jesus had everyone sit down, He blessed the food and had the disciples start handing it out. When everyone had their fill Jesus had the disciples collect the leftovers. There were seven basketfuls. Still the Pharisees among them came and asked Jesus for a sign from heaven. As if seven basketfuls of leftovers wasn't enough. But maybe, like me, you are thinking, Of course the Pharisees would get it wrong. But guess what happens as Jesus and His crew hop in the boat to travel to the other side?

The human part of Jesus had to be reflecting on the conversation with the Pharisees and perhaps He was frustrated. Meanwhile, the disciples were having their own conversation when Jesus warned them about the yeast of the Pharisees and Herod. Just like everyone at the T-ball game questioned why dad was sending one of our guys into the other team's dugout, the disciples wondered what Jesus meant by His warning. Of all the leftovers they'd only brought along one loaf. They wondered if perhaps Jesus was hinting, they should've brought more.

Jesus was fully aware of their conversation and launched into a series of questions. I imagine He wanted to ask them using the same tone my dad asked me about my math homework. I am sure Jesus wanted to pick them up and shake them like my dad picked me up by the arm one night and passionately asked, "How could you possssssibly not understand?" I had given him the same confused look the disciples must've given Jesus. So Jesus asked them, "Don't you remember feeding the five thousand with just five loaves? How many baskets were left over that night?" They answered, "Twelve." "And tonight, when I broke the seven loaves for four thousand, how many baskets were left over?" I imagine they looked at each other, still confused, but confirmed it was seven. Jesus looked at them and simply asked, "Do you still not understand?" If the disciples, the handpicked Holy Roller posse of Jesus, didn't see that He was the God of more than enough, I'm going to remind us, it's OK when we miss the call, when we don't see the signals, when we question what's next.

I don't think it's an accident the very next story is about a blind man. For we, the body of believers well over two thousand years removed from the walking and talking Messiah, are still going to be a little unclear and make mistakes.

I have a friend who talks about the process of a child learning to walk. He asks—when a toddler attempts a first few steps and then falls down—what parent says, "Oh, I've seen better?" In the same way, God is with us for each step of our faith journey. God is nearby when we are crawling around and wrestling with coming to believe in Him. Jesus is with us as we hang ourselves on the cross of doing things our way. The Holy Spirit is sustaining us as we stumble around and stub our toes on the base of each stony distraction laid out to trip us up.

Are you in a dust cloud? Was there a play at the plate? Do you feel like the catcher who's just been run over? Are you checking to make sure your head is attached and appendages still move? Or are you feeling like the batter who has used his third strike? No matter what it is, it's OK. Fortunately, the game of a lifetime spent trying to be more like Jesus comes with way more than just three strikes. Take a moment, orient yourself, and get your bearings. But start looking for your coach.

When we experience loss, the kind of loss that makes us ache, I promise God is close by. God hears our groaning hearts. God is close to the broken and the oppressed. He's in the midst of our racial, religious, and relationship tensions. He's on the corner and in the dark alleys with the addict. He's knocking at the hearts of those with plenty as if to point out those who have little. He walks through the prison walls and serves those serving time. He's with the bag of food you purchased and gave to the beggar at the stop sign. He hears the prayers of the mother or father whose baby didn't make it. He's with the widowed, the spouse who's been left or betrayed, and He's faithfully pursuing the spouse who did the leaving or betraying.

My dad, the coach who marched onto the field and sent his catcher into the opposing team's dugout, recognized the need to balance the tension between two forces. And I bet he'd encourage you to not beat yourself up when you miss the signs and blinking signals—and at the same time to not be paralyzed by inaction and remain in the dugout doing nothing. I'm really glad my dad was able to be my coach for T-ball. And likewise, our heavenly Father is our eternity coach. He's got the game plan, He knows all the positions. He's encouraging, upbeat, and cheering us on, even when we feel like we've been tagged out or struck out for the umpteenth time. He always sees us. He sees when we score and when we sit and sulk. He knows we are going to blow it, but most importantly He knows the final score. And each and every day, He's still inviting us to play ball.

CHAPTER 6

How Can I Get There from Here?

G rowing up in a Catholic church is a unique experience. When
the church is in southwest Virginia, the experience is next level.
Our Lady of Nazareth was a small parish, and I can still remember
the frantic Sunday morning drive from our house to 824 Campbell
Avenue. Mom and Dad would sleep in, which, in hindsight, is
understandable: my parents were busy enough raising three kids
and trying to figure out how to own and operate their business.
But the extra sleep typically meant we were running behind. This
meant on Sunday mornings, we were a family of five in a stock car
race.

Our station wagon was the epitome of what comes to mind
when you think 1970s family vehicle. Right down to the fake wood
paneling on the sides, overlaying the ever-so-unique yellowish
color. It was awesome whenever we made the seven-hour trip to

see family in Pennsylvania because it had the seat in the rear. You know the one: it would flip up and allow a passenger to sit in the wayback, facing backwards. This was handy for getting a trucker to blast his horn.

Ours also had an eight-track player. To my dad's credit, he became skilled at precisely knowing the point to change the track, to have effectively rewound, and replay a favorite song. But Sunday mornings were no vacation, we were a family of five charging to church.

There was no music on those mornings. Unless you count the choruses of "Are you ready?", "Do we have to go?", and "Get into the car!" as lyrics or music. Usually in a rush, most of us with half-brushed hair and maybe-brushed teeth. Seat belts, you ask? What are those for? Besides, on Sunday mornings the hump seat was the best. It was way more fun to slide across the back seat and smoosh your sister into the door because Dad was making a turn as if entering the back stretch at Daytona Speedway. There are limited memories on Campbell Avenue, because soon the church was building a new facility on Electric Road. Yes, it's a real road in Roanoke and yes, we did pretend our church was on "Electric Avenue" when Eddie Grant released his song in 1982.

I will never forget the early evening when Mom and Dad drove us out to the build site. It was cool to walk inside the church as it was being built. The roof was on, and the bricks of the gathering space floor had been laid. The square granite structure that would become the bubbling baptismal font was already in place, minus the water. Overhead were four skylights, allowing light from the heavens to spill in and fill the otherwise empty space.

This place stood in stark contrast to all the other Catholic churches I'd ever seen. Mom and Dad said there would be no kneelers, not even pews—just simple cushioned seats for us to sit in. Aside from the skylights, this would be a windowless church. No stained-glass depictions to gaze into whenever the priest's homily got boring. Don't get me wrong, I really liked the priest we had. Father Tom was a great guy, loved God and us kids. There was something sincere and heartfelt in everything he did.

Eventually the church building was completed. We still had the same Daytona race to Sunday service, just to a different building. Instead of going straight up the hill by what was Community Hospital, we now made a left-hand turn onto the newly extended 581/Route 220. The on ramp made it feel even more like we were exiting the pits and racing to full speed. While it was a new space, it was the same race. We'd arrive just in time or a little late.

● ● ●

Because I didn't quite fully understand Father Tom's talks after the gospel reading, I went to church for one reason. OK, maybe two.

Maybe, like you, I was pretty much bored at church as a kid. One of the things I would do to pass the time was watch Father Tom during the parts of the service he wasn't doing himself. The lectors of the first and second reading would each take their turn reading scripture to the congregation. All the while, I'd have my eyes on Father Tom. He'd sit in his chair, the one with the tall back and armrests. Sometimes he'd prop up his chin or the side of his face with a fist or open hand. Occasionally, he'd even sit there with his eyes closed. A-ha, I thought, church is so boring even Father Tom is taking a nap! I even shared this observation once with my parents.

Aside from parental persuasion, one of the main reasons I did enjoy church was when the service was over. No sarcasm, because after church, we'd all gather in the fellowship hall. The grownups would talk with other grownups, but the kids got doughnuts. These were the good kind from the local doughnut shop. We are talking big doughnuts, all kinds: plain, powdered, sprinkled, blueberry, jelly, lemon, even chocolate-filled. Talk about manna from heaven!

Even Father Tom would join us and frequently be seen enjoying a coffee, a doughnut, and conversation. It was during one of these more relaxed moments my parents were talking with Father Tom. He was older than my parents but seemed younger than my grandparents. I remember he always had white hair and was appropriately friendly. On this occasion, Dad asked me to share my observation with Father Tom. At first, I tried to play dumb, as if I didn't know what Dad was talking about. Was he really asking me to call the guy out? Right to his face? I didn't know much about God at this point but felt for sure if you are calling out a priest, right to his face, well, this would have to be one of those things my Polish, Catholic grandmother says, puts you on the Hell Express. With some coaxing, I did eventually share how it looked like he was as bored at church as I was. His expression surprised me.

His smile and laugh were not what I was expecting. But then he said, "You know sometimes I probably do get distracted if a baby is crying or people are moving." Just as I thought he was confirming my suspicions, he added, "But I am not bored when I am listening or asleep if I close my eyes. That's when I am trying extra hard to listen for what God wants to say to me."

I think in some way he was forgiving me for being bored at church or thinking he was asleep—and at the same time encouraging me in a very kind way to pay attention at church. This stuck with me. With his white hair and the fact that we called him Father Tom, I thought he maybe was God, or at least a distant cousin. It struck me as refreshingly honest and sincere when he admitted sometimes it's hard to listen and hear what God might be saying to us. Shortly after our talk over doughnuts there was another incident, and I was glad Father Tom was listening for God with his eyes closed.

● ● ●

When Mom and Dad had two more girls, we older kids were often enlisted to help. And I am not just talking about cleaning up baby toys, holding, or feeding them. This Sunday morning was no different. The race was on, and we just had more of us scrambling to get ready and hop in the car. Mom had fed and dressed the baby, and I had drawn the duty of watching her and keeping her safe. She was a cute kid, and I was over my silly disappointment of not having a brother. This didn't mean I didn't roughhouse a little. We were having fun and then the smell hit me. I knew I hadn't passed gas and since she was the only other one in the room, I was hoping she had. To my chagrin, she had passed gas and a whole lot more. Suddenly, I was in charge of an entirely different kind of duty.

It was the kind of mess requiring multiple wipes and an entirely new outfit. She didn't seem to mind. In fact, she was cheerful and giggling as I held my breath and grimaced. I was not happy. I changed the outfit as best I could, just hoping it would pass Mom's inspection. I placed a fresh diaper on her and then I thought, OK, little one, this is where I will get my revenge. I spotted the baby powder and let's just say I liberally applied. It was less about revenge and more an attempt to clear the air. She was dressed just in time, and all of us were off to church.

When we arrived the only available seats were directly in front of the choir. Mom wasn't too thrilled to be sitting on the front row, but it's what was left. The only other option was for us to stand in the lobby and listen over the speakers. I was OK with front row seats. Partly because of the music, but this also gave me the perfect spot to watch Father Tom. He was again propping up his head, but this time I knew what he was doing when his eyes closed. I did not, however, see what my little sister was doing.

She was at the age where she could crawl and sit up but couldn't walk just yet. She had mastered grasping furniture and standing for a bit and when I glanced over, that's exactly what she was doing. Maybe I smiled and waved or perhaps she was distracted but, in her excitement, she raised her hand, lost her balance, and plopped directly onto her bottom. Have you ever been to a concert or maybe a middle school dance? Do you remember the fun and excitement when the smoke machine would surge to life and fill the space with the mystical white smoke? That image would accurately describe what happened the moment she landed.

The extraneous powder I had earlier applied exited out each side of her diaper. My mouth dropped open, and I started to laugh. My little sister was perplexed and looked about with a grin on her face. My mother, however, did not have the same happy grin. It did not take her long to surmise who was responsible. I had shared the diaper challenge with her but in this moment the weight of her stare cut through the haze like a strobe light. Oh sure, we can laugh about it now, but right then I didn't think she would be consoled or forgive me if I pointed out Father Tom was "listening for God" and not watching the billowing smoke-show diaper.

Doughnuts and diapers aside, the other reason I enjoyed church was the music! Picture the early '80s with a talented full band leading worship. I mean it had everything: awesome lead vocals, both male and female, acoustic and on occasion electric guitars, a man who could slap a bass so smooth, and piano playing that danced on every ivory, bringing to life the music from the hymnal. Even my Babci appreciated this lively music. Today you might call it praise and worship. From my recollection this music would give even our contemporary artists a run for their money.

●　　●　　●

But it wasn't about a sound, or a particular vocalist or instrument. It was about worshiping this thing we called God. There was a portion of the service where the singing was a back-and-forth between the prayers of the priest and the response of the people. It all ended with an "Our Father, Forever."

I'm embarrassed I don't have words to convey the sound or how it could make a preteen like me feel somehow connected to something much bigger than me in this pew-less, stained glass–less version of a Roman Catholic church. I wasn't completely sure why I felt connected. All I knew was, occasionally the music was so good it made my dad cry. I didn't think guys cried but I felt it too. It wasn't about pews, kneelers, stained glass, or statues. It was something different altogether. It was freeing and forgiving.

The cumulative positive experiences led me to contemplate what heaven would be like.

How would you answer the question? When I was a child, I thought it would be one really long church service. Maybe what you were told has you thinking of angels on clouds playing harps? The dad of one of my college friends (a fellow alum of the university we attended) would always tell us, "Well, of course there has to be balloons in heaven, and you can catch up with me by the blue and gold balloons." As I got older, I developed a habit of asking people I met the following question: What are the three things you hope are in heaven?

Over the years, I've been given some good answers. Some I agree with and others I would've never thought of including. An Olympic gold-medalist swimmer said he hopes to see his dogs. A wrestling coach of mine said good coffee. Others have told me they hope to be reunited with friends or family members. Another person wants a certain kind of tree and plenty of stocked fishing ponds. Several mentioned the feeling of a grand party; maybe that's where the balloons will be. I really hope there is something like music—maybe from those days at our church on Electric Road, maybe it's the angels and harps, or maybe it's the Big Band–era my Babci listened to. But I think there must be something like music to help us worship and thank the guy who made sure we were invited. Oh, and of course jelly doughnuts. They probably have those up there too, right? Far and away the number one answer came with different words but had something to do with knowing they'd been forgiven and experiencing a whole lot of God's grace. All the answers and anything you would add to the list sound good to me, but it's the last two I find most interesting. Grace and forgiveness called me deeper, beyond thinking what heaven will be like to how can I get there.

I know I'm not the first to admit this, but as a human, I screw it up. Our love is imperfect, we lie to protect ourselves or others, we fall short, hurt others, and even take shots at our relationship with God. And while we don't always know the ways to avoid these, we are smart enough to know we need to experience God's grace and forgiveness when we think of heaven. Instead of smoke and mirrors, Jesus used love and forgiveness. If there is anything Jesus taught, it would be how to love. The biggest part of how Jesus taught love involves extending grace and forgiveness to each other. When He was asked about how many times we are supposed to forgive someone, Jesus said we are to forgive seventy-seven times. While the math implies a specific answer, most of us trying to be more like Jesus recognize it goes far beyond any number.

Fortunately, while He was here with us, Jesus loved and lived forgiveness in several ways. He liked to use stories to make His point about forgiveness, and sometimes the story showed us what not to do. During a conversation with Peter, Jesus told a story of an unforgiving servant. He also shared hope-filled stories, like the crippled woman who spent years bent over and was suddenly able to stand straight because Jesus forgave her. The story of the lost sheep assures us that when we get off the path and sin, He will pursue and forgive us. And of course, the love of the father and the way he forgave not only his prodigal son but the one who'd remained with him.

Jesus forgave those who directly sinned against Him. After the soldiers scourged and nailed Him to the cross, Jesus prayed, "Father, forgive them." After He'd risen from the dead, rather than disown Peter for denying Him, Jesus entered the room where Peter had hidden with the other disciples. Rather than lecture them, He offered forgiveness and peace three times. Once for each of Peter's denials.

But Jesus also forgave those who had sinned against others. He told the paralytic, "Child, your sins are forgiven." When a sinful woman bathed His feet with her tears and wiped them with her hair, He said, "Your sins are forgiven." One of my favorites is the woman caught in adultery. The elders sought to trick Jesus, but He said whoever is without sin can cast the first stone. Then He knelt to the ground, doodled in the dirt, and waited. One by one they left until it was Jesus and the woman. He said, "I do not condemn you." Even at the very end as Jesus was dying on the cross, He assured the repenting criminal, "Today you will be with me in paradise."

Father Tom allowed me to learn about something more valuable than doughnuts or music. He forgave me for thinking he was asleep. My mother and sister forgave me for using too much powder. But things change as we get older; hurts and betrayals can get bigger. Forgiving others is no easy step. Take heart—Jesus knows. He was partly human like us. Forgiving those who've hurt us is not our first instinct; it's not a natural response. But forgiving others truly is the only response we can have in the light of His encompassing love for us. Jesus assured us we can forgive them. He gave us His authority to do so. It won't come easy. There might be months or years we choose to hold the acid in our hands and heart. While they may not be our first choices, we know love and forgiveness are the right ones.

CHAPTER 7

Truth and Peace

One of the best sick days I ever confabulated was a day the cafeteria served hotdogs, peanuts, and snickerdoodles. We had the choice between white or chocolate milk and I went with chocolate. Our lunchtime was some ridiculous hour well before noon and I had determined I'd had enough of school for the day.

I was eating my hotdog and immediately added some peanuts. I paused to consider the consistency of what was in my mouth. This was exactly the sort of thing our school custodian would pour the ever so uniquely smelling, odor-absorbing powder over when a kid got sick. I swallowed and cleansed my palate with some milk. Then traded away my snickerdoodle for more peanuts. In our elementary school economy, snickerdoodles were like gold bars. I traded half of my snickerdoodle to two different kids for their peanuts. They couldn't believe I wanted to trade away a snickerdoodle, and this worked right into my plan. I said, "I just don't think I feel so good."

I took a big bite of my hot dog, chewing it as carefully as I could. It had to look like I had tried to eat but I wanted it to have some chunkage. I didn't swallow it. Then carefully avoiding detection, I nonchalantly packed in my mouth the double portion of peanuts. I thought my mouth was about to burst. As I chewed it occurred to me, I should add some milk for dramatic effect. With cheeks as full as any chipmunk, I filled any remaining void in my mouth with milk. As I put my milk back in its designated spot on the school lunch tray, I gave it all a good swish in my mouth and thought, Time to go home.

I pushed my chair back from the table as I began to spew the concoction in my mouth. I was careful to get some on the tray but not any of my classmates. The rest went on the floor underneath my table. The resulting eruption of kids avoiding my Mount Vesuvius of food was effective. The next thing I knew one of the teachers was walking me down the hall toward the main office. Our custodian must've already been alerted as we passed each other in the hallway. And in a little while, I suspected, my mom would collect me from school, tuck me in bed, and bring me some soda and crackers.

●   ●   ●

I know the three of us were a handful, and I'm probably imagining this, but it seemed like Mom was always angry with me more than she was with the girls. Of course, episodes like this did not help the times I truly was sick. I have significant damage in my left ear. In fact, when I was hired decades later to teach in the same school district, I had the dubious distinction of qualifying as a "disabled hire." I can't remember if they said it was a 40 percent loss and 60 percent good or vice versa, but clearly it was significant. Oddly, it's only in a certain pitch range. I know if I am lying on the couch watching television, I can hear much better with my right ear. (Ironically, I can still hear my cell phone even when it is vibrating in the other room.) There are plenty of things that could explain the hearing loss in my left ear: sinus problems, ear infections, or my prolific use of stereo headphones. Most of my ailments were legitimate. Mostly.

Dr. Myer was my pediatrician for as long as I can remember; I really liked him. He seemed like a nice man who wanted to help people get better. As I got older, I was clearly one of his oldest patients. We laughed when he did one of my sports physicals. I can remember when he checked my reflexes. After checking my ears and gagging me with an oversized Popsicle stick, he stood in front of me and tapped my knee with the hard rubber mallet hammer. Involuntarily, the smack of the mallet launched my leg his way. So much so my foot moved the long white medical coat he was wearing. I recall the surprised look on his face as he humorously said, "I think I'll stand over here for the next leg."

On this occasion, however, we were there because of continuing headaches. I did not currently have a sinus infection, but my head really did hurt. I was sitting on the crinkly white butcher paper when Dr. Myer asked me some questions about hallucinogenic something or another. I must've had the quizzical tilted head look puppies give. I looked at my mom and she asked, "He wants to know if you've taken any drugs."

I thought, What, drugs? Me? Woah, woah, woah what is happening? This was way beyond any sort of plot to get out of school. I started to cry as I responded, "No, Mom, no, not ever." Dr. Myer remained calm and, as always, said and did the right thing. Some blood work was ordered, tests interpreted, and a short time after that I was being admitted to the hospital for further tests and observations.

My fifth-grade mind was boggled. I couldn't comprehend what was happening. And this was one of many times my mother selflessly showed her more loving side. The hospital room was fun and terrible at the same time. There was a color TV and the bed adjusted with the push of a button. Those were the perks. The food, terrible. The hospital gown, drafty. Between my fashionable attire and navigating the IV drip bag on wheels, even going to the bathroom was an event. This was not a fun escape from school. I was scared. Not to mention all the nurses who came throughout the day to draw blood. There was one I referred to as Dracula after Mom told me she would come and take my blood while I was asleep. Mom told her my nickname for her and she very kindly said she understood and tried to explain it was to help figure out what was wrong so they could get me better. I still tried to sleep with one eye open.

Eventually the words hepatitis and migraines were mentioned. I didn't know what it meant but it became obvious this meant more time in the hospital. As if a hospital stay for a child wasn't depressing enough, it just so happened that I would be in for my birthday. I was grateful for the occasional hamburger with only mustard my Dad would sneak into my hospital room. I couldn't help but feel special when the school sent over a card signed by all my classmates. I could've done without the homework, but it was something to do other than lying in bed all day.

● ● ●

I don't recall exactly how long I stayed in the hospital, but I do not recall a single time waking up in the day or night and my mom not being there. I don't know how she did it. But I do know why. She, in her own way, as best she could, loved me. She would prove this again and again. Like she did shortly after Christmastime when we three oldest kids were still little.

Santa decided a dart board would be a good gift for us. Yes, I said a dart board—you know, the thing with the sharp, needle-like projectiles frequently referred to as missiles. The barroom sport derived from archery in which contestants throw said missiles at a circular seventeen and three-quarter inch–wide board trying to score points. Something tells me Dad negotiated this one with "Saint Nick." I bet he used the "it will improve their hand-eye coordination" theory. It was Dad who hung it up on a two-by-four stud in our roughed-in, but mainly unfinished basement. I'm sure it seemed safe enough and there was the warning to be careful. Apparently, my younger sister didn't listen.

We missed the board more often than we hit it, but this allowed us to establish our own safety protocols. We'd stand near the roughed-in door to what would eventually become the furnace room, as this was directly behind the dart board. We'd loudly proclaim. "I'm going in," and to the three of us kids, the eldest barely past ten, it was code for an all-out cease-fire. Except the one day when it was my turn to collect our errant throws.

I made the agreed-upon declaration and pulled open the door. Dad—being so busy trying to run a restaurant—hadn't had time to install the doorknob yet. This is where everything started to occur in slow motion. I took one step inside. Suddenly there was a piercing pain in my upper right thigh. I looked down, just imagining what could cause such pain. Dad had warned us about the possibility of exposed nails, but I had yet to bump into one. Maybe this was the first. Eventually my eyes located and determined the source.

The yellow plastic body and fins of the dart were sticking straight out of my thigh as if it were a bicyclist arm indicating an impending left-hand turn. I heard my youngest sister utter an "Ooops!" And in an instant, I felt she would experience a pain of her own. As I reached out to grasp and remove the dart, I heard her running for the stairs. I cried out, "Oh my God!"

The needle came out with only a little blood. In the next heartbeat I was on her trail chasing her up the stairs, screaming, "I said I was going in!" and repeating "I'm going to kill you!" Perhaps because of all the screaming, Mom appeared from behind the door at the top of the stairs just in time for my sister to dart between the door frame and my mom's leg, which was now attempting to block the door and shield my little sister.

"What is going on?" Mom asked. I simply produced the dart with the inch-long needle which still had biological evidence trickling down. Fortunately, Mom knew what to say and do to calm me down. She acknowledged I was right, which was refreshing. My sister did survive the day, but we didn't play darts much more after that.

● ● ●

What stuck with me were two things: first, the importance of telling the truth, and second, it's good to be a peacemaker.

As a child, I saw faking illnesses as a way to spend time with Mom, enjoy being taken care of, and, yes, my fifth-grade mind thought maybe I could get her to like me more. But generally speaking, moms tend to like their kids and would do anything for them. My mom did so by living in the hospital and keeping me out of jail by stopping me from killing my sister on dart day. I recognize this isn't the case for everyone. Part of telling our truth means getting in touch with what happened.

Let me start by stating this: if you've been hurt by your mom, your dad, or anyone else, it was wrong. We know scars don't just show up physically. Some of us carry emotional, psychological, and/or other scars that aren't always obvious on the surface. Hear me say this: I am truly sorry for what you experienced. No abuse is OK. Fortunately, the tide is changing as it relates to abuse and mental health. The stigmas are disappearing, and treatments are more readily accessible. If you need help, there are options listed in the back of this book. Seek the help you need.

Jesus also offers to help us. In fact, He promised us that if we ask, it will be given. If we seek, we will find. And if we knock, the door will be opened. I will admit to the fact I'm guilty of taking His words and relegating Him to being a genie in a lantern. We've all avoided telling the truth. We rationalize little lies to ourselves or to others. And while sometimes we try to justify our half-truths by saying we didn't want to hurt someone, who are we really deceiving? Jesus didn't dance around the truth and He's not blue. It is, however, true. We "ain't never had a friend like" Him. Jesus was talking to His friends when He said, "I am the way the truth and the life."

Another way of thinking about this could be: He is the way to find the truth and get to our real life with God. Our truth is simple. More than a sick day in bed, more than our mother's love, more than a Lamborghini or anything out of the genie's bottle, more than mansions, millions of dollars, more than social media influence—we all want peace.

Jesus had a way of turning the things upside down. And sometimes we'd be wise to follow that example. George Costanza was a character in the television show Seinfeld; one of this character's multiple challenges involved romantic relationships. At one point he concluded every instinct he'd ever had had been wrong and decided to do the opposite.

In one scene his friend told him an attractive woman was looking at him. He responded by pointing out that attractive women don't look at men who are unemployed and live at home with their parents. His instinct was to ignore the woman who looked his way. But because of his declaration to do the opposite, he approached her. In this episode of the show, doing the opposite works for a while but the character ends up in trouble.

We don't live in a TV show. We aren't characters. We are real people with real hurts. Protecting ourselves often takes precedence over an inconvenient truth. But perhaps we can learn something from Costanza after all.

Maybe our past does have real hurts. And maybe out of those hurts we want to justify holding on to or acting out of our anger because, after all, someone hurt us. We could go one step further and find that time when Jesus flipped over those tables. Jesus was not advocating literally flipping out. What Jesus said, and more often showed, was how peacemakers are blessed. It's true we all want peace, but it's not our instinct to seek it out. As a child, I taunted my siblings. As an athlete, I made my competitions a personal conflict. Even today our world is filled with conflicts and wars. But that's not how God wants us to live.

My mother wasn't perfect, and neither was yours. We make some interesting choices. I think my mother tried to remind me of this, the day my sister darted my leg. Somehow, she validated my anger, my emotions, my feelings, and helped spare the life of my sister. She showed me that just like the characters on television, we all have our flaws. She was right. I faked being sick to get out of school. My sister ignored me when I went behind the dartboard. I made it worse when I said I wanted to kill her. I'm not trying to make light of the bigger hurts we've experienced, just mentioning a few lesser ones and acknowledging our bigger ones aren't easy to talk about. The good news is when we seek truth and peace, we end up finding hope and maybe the physician who knows a thing or two about our hurts.

CHAPTER 8

Being Broken

Dentist. The mere mention of the occupation generally elicits one of two reactions. Whether it's cavities, crooked, or impacted teeth, most people do not look forward to their biannual dental visit. I am one of the outliers. When I was younger my dentist told me I had really good teeth. That's not to say I didn't have a cavity or two, and there was a phase when I over-brushed and actually messed up my gums. But I got lucky, and all thirty-two teeth came in perfectly straight. Because of this I was spared the metallic fate of many of my friends—braces.

When my sister had to get braces, it was fascinating to learn how they work. They glue metal brackets to each tooth and string a wire to connect them all. The process exerts a gentle but constant force to gradually align the teeth. Maybe you are like some of my friends who had to have their wisdom teeth pulled. If you've ever ~~enjoyed a laugh or~~ two from watching, or starring in, a video of a teenager post oral surgery, you should thank Dr. Morton.

William T. G. Morton was a young dentist in Boston during the mid-1800s. He was searching for a more effective way to sedate patients. Nitrous oxide was the drug of choice then and it's still used today for minor work. But Morton needed something more for his patients who required major work. He experimented with ether and found it successful for things like pulling teeth. Soon he was working with a surgeon and together the two performed the first major surgery where a patient inhaled and went under.[1] I didn't know it then, but I'd experience this "going to sleep" the day my sister and I were playing football in my grandparents' yard.

•   •   •

After living in Pennsylvania for most of their lives, my mom's parents moved to Virginia to be closer to us. They lived on a gravel path called Jordan Town Road. Their yard had two big trees and a stump perfectly situated as bases when we'd play "tenni-ball". It was our version of baseball except we used rackets and tennis balls. It was great for home runs and batting averages, not so much for a pitcher's ego. But summer was behind us. With the change of season, it had turned cooler. Accordingly, our game changed to football. What started out as burning off some of our sugar high from the sweet treats Babci provided us, eventually became a game. My oldest sister had scored on a play I'm sure would've been overturned if instant replay had existed back then. She threw off the ball. We used throw-offs instead of kickoffs because neither of us were very good at kicking. And our grandfather was not too fond of us using our heel to create a divot in his yard to serve as a tee.

Her throw caught the branches and knocked off some of the remaining leaves. The ball fell well short of coming to me. In fact, I would say it was slightly closer to me by just a few feet. In our league this meant one thing. Whoever got to the ball first would have possession. Our eyes locked and the sprint was on. Like two

[1] See footnote in Appendix

61

drivers in a demolition derby, we charged to get to the ball. My sister was older and still a little faster than me, but not by much. As we approached the ball, I determined the only way I would get there first was with a Pete Rose–inspired headfirst slide.

I watched as my left arm started to possess the familiar yellow and blue Nerf football. It had only a chunk or two missing from where our dog had played with it. I saw her body sort of mimicking my slide but with a twisting move as if to shield me from getting the ball. I had to admit, it was a good idea on her part, but I was still determined to get the ball. I heard a crack, then another, and felt pain more significant than the yellow dart piercing my thigh. I gave up the ball, pulled my arm in toward my stomach and rolled around on the ground for the drama. Like most kids do at the slightest scrape, I was yelling, "It's broke, it's broke!" I was half making my case for a penalty (or at least a do-over) and half realizing something was truly wrong. I heard my sister say, "Yeah right, get up, it's my ball." I only remember a few things after that. First and foremost, glancing down to see my arm.

It was no longer straight as it had been just moments before. I blinked, hoping there was some dirt, a twig, or a leaf in my eye. I opened my eyes and while there were no bones breaking the skin, I now had a "step." We'd later learn both the ulna and radius had been broken during the play. Apparently, one moved under the other to deform my arm and cause the step-like feature. I wasn't imagining this; it was really broken.

I don't believe for a second my sister meant any harm. It was a hustle play, and any possible sign of nefarious intent disappeared the moment I lifted my arm to show her. I remember her mouth opening and all the color fading from her face. She disappeared into my grandparents' house and the next thing I knew we were in the back of Dadzi's car. He was up front driving, Babci and I were in the back seat. My head was in her lap. No seat belts, but by this time I was entering a state of shock. I don't remember much of what was going on and even less of what I was saying, but Babci would.

I do remember my parents met us along Route 24 in the turnoff to our neighborhood. Rather than move me they just swapped cars. Eventually we arrived at Roanoke Community Hospital. I can remember a male nurse or orderly lifting me onto a bed. I suppose he might have administered some pain med, but I don't remember. I do recall feeling pain and the moment the doctor on duty came into the room.

He was Asian and spoke in broken English. It would be the same doctor who years later would stitch up a busted chin I'd get playing a high school football game. But on this trip to the ER, his focus was my broken bones and that "step" in my arm. He took one look and said, "Oh, this very bad, but no bones out." He tried to set the bones, and I let out a scream. The nice guy who helped me onto this bed was still there and he said to me, "Just squeeze my hand when it hurts." Two more tries to set the bones and two more screams later, the nice guy said, "Hey, how about you try squeezing this bed rail instead." After another futile attempt to set the arm and one more scream, I was moved to an operating room.

The doctor informed my parents it would be best to set the arm while I was under. By this time, I was lying down on the gurney. I heard the doctor's voice and saw his now-familiar eyes and glasses peering from behind a medical mask. There was one of those big operating lights overhead. I could hear beeping and the sounds of other people in the room. My vision was blurry, but I could tell none of them were family.

I tried to lift my head and look around to see what was going on when this hand gently grasped my head and placed it back down. The head attached to the arm would appear upside down with the same medical gear on as everyone else in the room. I was startled but heard the Asian doctor's voice tell me the man was going to give me some air to help me to feel better.

The anesthesiologist's plastic mask covered my face for a moment. A female voice told me to relax and breathe deeply. The faces and overhead light were flickering up and down as if the vertical control on the television at our house needed adjusting. I blinked to clear my vision but no luck, still flickering. I blinked again convinced this time it would work, and it did. Well, sort of anyway.

My eyes opened and I was on my side. My dad was there. He called my name, told me I was in the recovery room, and the doctors had put me under to fix my arm. Oh yeah, my arm. I went to lift it to see if the step was gone. It was, but replaced with a cast. Soon I was back in a regular room and held overnight for observation. I was feeling less groggy and drinking a soda when Babci arrived. She'd been the first responder who held me in the back of her car and was relieved to see I was feeling better. But as grandmothers will do, she didn't miss an opportunity.

"Oh, Kevin," she said, "I know you say you don't like going to church and how it's so booooring." She did a mostly accurate interpretation of my frequent description of church. She continued by asking, "But who was it you cried out to in your moment of need?" My face must've revealed I genuinely did not know the answer to her question. After a pause she resumed her impersonation of me by holding her own arm and adding, "As I held you in the back of the car all you could say was 'Oh God, oh God!' You see, even though you say you're bored, He came to you when you cried out."

I shook my head as the room erupted in laughter. Score one for Polish Catholic grandmothers. My break eventually healed and after having my fifth-grade friends sign it, the day finally came to have it removed. I did take a little pleasure knowing I would be getting out of school and not have to pretend being sick.

I asked if I could keep the cast. It had literally been a part of me for two months. I had to cover it in plastic to bathe and even though it was on my non-dominant hand, simple things took a little getting used to. Things like tying my shoes, buttoning my clothes, and adjusting my belt. Even fun things like playing outside—all had to be slightly modified. To me the cast was like a treasure chest of memories. Eventually though, Mom helped me see I didn't need the cast to hold on to memories or the lessons learned.

●　　●　　●

You see, just like real pirate treasure chests that have been buried underground or deep in saltwater, the cast was also full of dirt and sweat. It stunk. So we threw it out.

The cast is gone, but every now and then I am reminded about the importance of calling out to God. Before this football mishap, I typically only prayed when things seemed broken. But didn't we all do this when we were younger? And if we're being honest, maybe we still do it more often than we'd like to admit.

How is it, in this information based, twenty-four–hour news cycle, social media interconnected world, we've never been so disconnected and isolated? Well, at least until March of 2020, when we and the entire world had to take isolation to an entirely different level.

Don't get me wrong, some good things came out of the recent pandemic. Many of us reexamined our personal and work life balance. Maybe you were one of those who worked fifty to sixty or more hours a week, and then added in being a homemaker, coaching, or even just transporting your children to their activities. For years, I was one of those. For whatever reason, we choose to ignore or not listen to the adage less is more. The idea was first mentioned in a poem back in Dr. Morton's day. And not surprisingly Jesus had already flipped this around and showed us we can do more with less through relationships.

Jesus's entire message focused on relationships. He often preached about the importance of relationship with our heavenly Father, but He also showed it by loving and investing in a select few to literally change the world. We humans are made for relationship. Once, Jesus was asked to summarize what was most important and His response pointed back to our need for relationships. He said love, meaning be in relationship with God. And secondly was also love, being in relationship with others in the same way we love ourselves. I think sometimes we mess this up.

Too often we take self-responsibility and self-reliance too far. These can be great things when kept in check. The problem comes when our practice of personal responsibility and self-reliance gets muddled with our old definitions of self. This is when we are more likely to wander into the land of self-centeredness, leaving us alone and isolated. Maybe this is why He told us the story of sheep who wander off. Living reliant on self isn't what Jesus talked about. Despite our tendency to lead a DIY life, we know we are better when we open our hearts to relationships—first and foremost, with the Father. God crafted each of us to be unique. But also in cooperation with our fellow humans. I learned the world doesn't need another professional football player, but that I do have much to offer. And guess what? The world needs what you have. All too often we shift from cooperation to competition. We do it in business, at work, and sadly, even in family at home, resulting in broken hearts and broken homes.

But let's not beat ourselves up too much. Adam and Eve messed up, the heroes of the faith and even the most loving disciples got distracted a time or two. And just like them, we tend to revert to self. Maybe, like me, you were taught as a child that if you break something, you need to do everything you can to fix it or make it right. What can we do to fix what's broken? How about we stop wherever we are and consider three things.

First, what was Jesus all about? Relationships. Rather than continuing down the road of self, let's stop. If we've lived any amount of time, we already know what it feels like when we are farthest off course. This is when we need to pause and trust our relationship with God.

Second, let's work to limit those things distracting us from the relationships Jesus said we should focus on the most. Again, we are likely to get off to a better start and persist in limiting our distractions when we first admit we are likely to screw it up. Even Peter got distracted. We don't have to eliminate everything we do in the name of self-care. But maybe we'd be wise to reexamine our "me time", and instead consider "we time." How we do this depends on our life. Married and single people are likely to have as varied and different needs as women and men. But let's remember what Peter learned during his walk and not get distracted. When we invest in our first relationship, the next steps and other relationships have a way of coming into focus.

Finally, let's be mindful of what we hold onto. When I was a kid, I really wanted that stinky old cast. And maybe, like me, you've held onto hurts far too long. I am not saying it's not cool to hold onto memories, but there comes a point when we have to move on, both from good times but especially from the hurts that left us broken. Mom was right. I didn't need the cast to remind me of the football game. And I would've been silly and wrong to hold a grudge.

The cast is long gone but every now and then I am still reminded about calling out and being heard. My Babci was right too. God heard my cry back then. He hears our cries and sees our broken things now. Especially the brokenness we don't like to talk about. It was impossible for me to fix my own arm. In the same way, it's impossible for us to live the life Jesus calls us to without the risk of being broken. Living a life in the pursuit of loving relationships inherently means we are both "all in" and we might get hurt too. But we can stand and be confident knowing it's the right thing because it's what He did and still does in His pursuit of each of us.

Games We Play

Growing up the only boy with four sisters certainly has its advantages. For example, I never got hand-me-down clothes. You might think it's an obvious one, but knowing how frugal my grandparents and parents were, let's just say I was greatly relieved. Of course, originally, I was the only boy planted in the middle of two sisters. When I was eleven, Mom was pregnant again. This was the early '80s and Mom's baby doctor arranged a visit where we could come in and listen to the baby's heartbeat. After my own hospital stays, I was still leery to be around anything remotely resembling hospitals and medical equipment—but this was different.

Mom was the patient—or was it the baby? I suppose it was both. Regardless, I was relieved it wasn't me. This was before today's current trend of gender reveal parties. The technology existed if parents really wanted to know ahead of time. But I remember my parents playing it more traditional and waiting to find out the day the baby was born. I recall Mom telling the doctor or nurses they did not want to know. Unfortunately, I also recall one of the nurses stating something like, "Hmmmmm, the baby's heartbeat is within this range, which typically might be a boy, but of course we won't know until the baby comes."

Well, this news was all I needed. With absolutely zero medical training, I wholeheartedly concluded the baby on the way just had to be a boy. I quickly started to envision all the things I'd get to do with a baby brother. However, those dreams were dashed a few months later when my third sister was born. I started to wonder if my parents were out to get me when once more, about a year later, sister number four came along. I do love my sisters, all of them. They are incredible, talented, and loving people. But growing up with four sisters had its disadvantages too.

The girls just wanted to play dolls. My oldest sister said I could play with the Ken doll and my parents got me a GI Joe, but it was more boring than church to me. It didn't help when it came to arguing either. I was taught boys can't hit girls. Well, let's just say it sure seemed like my sisters had a way of hearing the same message and taking it right up to the line, knowing there wasn't any risk of retribution. But then came the day in the backyard under the dogwood tree.

My oldest sister had been on me all day. I can't remember about what, exactly, and full disclosure when I say all day, it was probably more like the most recent twenty minutes. Well, there we were. I can remember her mouthing something to me, and I had just had it. If I couldn't tackle her, I'd throw something at her and maybe get her to leave me alone. And there it was, an old bicycle basket sitting out by our sandbox. I picked it up and turned around. She and I had to be a good fifteen, maybe twenty feet apart. I cranked back and let the basket fly. In the first moments of flight, I recall thinking, Hey, that's a pretty good toss, it's heading right at her. I even admired the angle and arc of flight, thinking this would be a great toss over to the first baseman if I was still playing baseball. In the next nanosecond, I thought, That is a really good toss, too good a toss, and is headed right for her head.

The second thought ended up being accurate. It landed on her head, and because of the amount of spin it dug past her hair and into her scalp. The next thing I recall there were tears from both of us. She was whisked off to get some stitches. I think this was the first time I can recall being responsible for intentionally injuring a person. I did not like the way this made me feel. It was wrong; I didn't need a lecture or a spanking to know it. I wish I could tell you this was the last sibling argument we ever had, but if you've had a brother or sister, you already know it wasn't.

●　　●　　●

My dad's sister had three boys, so whenever we got together it was the closest thing I had to brothers. My oldest cousin was just five years younger than me, the next was a year younger than him, and I think the youngest was seven years younger than me. Being older, I was bigger and stronger. This is what it must feel like to be the big brother. And boy, the fun we had playing games in the yard! Football, kickball, wiffleball, and this was the '80s, so there was plenty of Nintendo Baseball too.

I won't speak for all, but I think in general boys are just more physical. As evidence I offer the following from the exploits of me and my cousins. In football my cousins designated me all-time quarterback. I think it was because I was the oldest and maybe because the field we played on was within walking distance of where my dad played his games. I really wasn't especially good at quarterback, but being five years older meant I could throw it the farthest. They all enjoyed trying to catch the deep bombs we'd see the pros catch on television.

Kickball and wiffleball were generally played during the warmer months on a dusty baseball field across the street from the house my dad grew up in. Those games were competitive and very spirited. They featured disputed calls, grand proclamations of "Automatic out!" and more than one Billy Martin–inspired storming off the field. I recall those times with my cousins as just easier, more natural. Maybe it was because I was bigger than them. But maybe it was because the emotions and competitiveness were a shared, unspoken language. The holidays were the times we were together, and they went by far too quickly.

●　　●　　●

But even before I got extra sisters, while I was still the only boy, the younger and older brother, I was caught between two people I rarely fully understood. My parents did the best they could to run a business, have a family of three, and keep some sense of peace in a house full of kids. It doesn't matter if you grew up on the coast, in the north or in the south. If you've been a parent or a sibling, you know. That's hard, y'all!

Mom was typically the enforcer. I don't mean those words to be unfair, but she was primarily the one home with us kids. She had to deal with us in the trenches. Dad was working long hours, trying to develop staff, meet expectations and payroll. Dad typically had to follow up after the fireworks, and he did have some creative ways of dealing with the reports he heard from Mom.

Depending on the day of the week, two of us would inevitably get into some disagreement. Dad would frequently make us sit down at a table together; we'd have to look each other in the eyes. (Gross!) And as if this wasn't bad enough, he'd make us hold hands. (Gag!) Oh, the little kid agony of not only looking at your sister—but having to hold her hand too? This had to be cruel and unusual punishment!

Once Dad attempted to relay a concept. He says he doesn't ever remember saying this but the message I heard was, "Put yourself in the other person's shoes." This was the best my brain could comprehend, his attempt to broker that day's peace treaty. I wonder if there isn't something to be learned in those words.

● ● ●

There's a story in the Bible when Jesus had some people do the exact same thing. As the story goes, there were some folks who first set up and then caught a lady in adultery. The first thing to bother me about this story is how we never hear about what happened to the guy the lady was caught with. Back then the punishment for adultery was literally stoning someone to death. But there is no mention of the man's fate. Makes me wonder. But they had caught the woman and the so-called religious experts thought they would test this Jesus character. Would He support the law of their faith, or would they have the evidence to show this popular young prophet was nothing but a scammer? Can't you picture the scene?

A scared, crying, shamed woman. Maybe she was literally tied to a post covered in rope or perhaps she was held firmly in a circle by whatever hurtful words the crowd spat upon her. Either way, there was no path for escape. There were two groups gathered this day. Those ready to hurl stones at her until she was dead and a group of onlookers ready to watch.

Jesus was also there. They attempted to trick Him into either condoning their actions or prove Himself a heretic. But this is precisely when Jesus thought outside the box (kind of like my dad was prone to do). After the "experts" asked their questions, rather than pick a side, Jesus simply crouched down. For a while, He ignored their questions. He simply took a finger and doodled in the dirt like a child. What started as a quiet, pregnant pause grew longer. I wonder what Jesus was thinking. Was He also wondering where the other portion of this adulterous act was? Was He entirely exhausted with the traps and games these people wanted to play? Did He hear whispers asking if this human race was worth the cost? I've heard some assert He was drawing words reminding the crowd of their own sins. I don't really know, but either way the crowd waited for an answer in what had to be an incredibly uncomfortable and awkwardly long silence, and I wonder—what exactly was Jesus thinking?

They say Jesus was equally human and divine. Based upon His recorded response it's easy to presume He was leaning on the divine, but I can't help but wonder what His human mind thought, what His heart felt in the moment. Eventually He did respond to them. He didn't use the guy lingo I and my cousins used. He didn't make Himself appear larger than life to deliver the kind of intimidating message a professional wrestler might send to an opponent. No, Jesus remained low to the ground. He kept drawing and simply, quietly, said, "Let him who has no sin, cast the first stone." You probably know what happened next.

When confronted by those hushed words and the reality of their hearts, one by one the stones fell, and the crowds all walked away. Can you see the scene unfold now? Jesus crouched low. How long did He stay there drawing in the dirt? How long did it take for the crowd's conviction to dismiss them? Can you see the woman? Perhaps she was in disbelief as to what had just happened. Eventually Jesus looked up, caught her eye, and quietly asked, "Where did they all go? Did no one condemn you?" She had to be scared. Who was this mystery man? Did He really not hear the thud of each stone being dropped? Did He not hear the grumbles of the crowd when confronted with the insinuation that they also had sins? Was He not paying attention? Did He really not hear or see them all walk away? How could He have missed it all? Maybe in disbelief, she stammered her response: "No one, sir." Did she worry about His response? Did she maybe think He was one of them and going to trick her? She didn't get the answers to her questions before He lovingly spoke these words to her: "Then neither do I. Go and leave your life of sin."

What happened next? Did she think to herself, Yeah, right, buddy—what's the catch? Did she say anything to Him or just quietly walk away? Something tells me there was a loving embrace of a Father and a daughter. If not an actual physical hug, there was surely love conveyed in His glance or maybe in the tone of His words. Maybe this is why I still hope in the moment, Jesus was more human than divine.

Because if He was, then it means each and every day, as humans we are also capable of the same kind of radical grace. Each of us is capable of giving and living in the total and complete level of forgiveness. We know it is already offered divinely. We can receive it for our own closely held secrets—whether it's an addiction, a personal failing, or other sins. And I can't help but wonder what might our world look like if we lived and dispensed this to each other on the same magnitude He did with her?

●　　●　　●

Yes, we must receive. But not only receive. We must also freely give away to those who have hurt us.

No rational human would ever endorse staying in an abusive situation. If you are hearing such a suggestion in my words, let me be clear: I am not. I am merely suggesting that holding on to our hurts in our heart is like trying to hold a raging fire in our hands. Our human heart was simply not designed to hold on to hurts. I think this might be why so many who have been wronged struggle when they find it hard to forgive. And perhaps this is the same reason why others can be heard verbally saying, "I forgive you" to the one who hurt them. They are not foolish or asking to be abused again; rather they have felt the sting. They know the burn of holding on to hurts. Maybe this is what Jesus meant when He told his disciples, "Those who have faith in me will do what I've done and even greater."

Where are you today? Do you still stand gripping the stones? What's the name on the stone? Is it Retribution, Payback, Hate, Envy? Or is it something more personal? Is it called "But he did this to me"? Or "She called me that"? Maybe you stand where the woman stood. Surrounded by accusers. Or maybe in today's world you think you've started a new life somewhere else. Maybe you thought you left all of this behind, but deep down inside you still feel surrounded. In the quiet moments before you drift off to sleep or just as you wake up, you admit to yourself that what you did was wrong.

Either way the guy doodling in the dirt is still here. He is still providing the same response He gave centuries ago. Can you hear it? Will you open the hands holding on to past hurt so they can receive His message? He said it to her back then. He is repeating it to us today. Open our eyes, Lord, help us to see your face. Open our ears, Lord, help us to hear your voice say, "Neither do I condemn you. Go now and leave your life of sin." Help us to move on in the hope and trust of your complete love for us. Open our hearts, too, Lord; help us to love like you.

CHAPTER 10

Go for Fresh Air

There are a great many things to cloud the thinking of a ten-year-old. Somewhere near the top of the list is when the county-wide fire drill is scheduled to occur at your school. In my school, fifth graders were the "seniors" of elementary school. We weren't those snot-nosed little kindergartners. We knew our way to the gym and the music room, and we even knew all the important grown-ups in school. As fifth graders we'd had all the teachers and they would smile and wave to us whenever our class was passing their class in the hall. With my penchant for coming up with illnesses to get out of school, I could've been on a first-name basis with Ms. Haldren in the front office, but of course even fifth graders don't call grown-ups by their first name. And then there was the principal, Mr. Stone.

As if his name wasn't intimidating enough, he was easily the tallest human being I'd seen in real life. The only people I'd seen taller than him were in The Guinness Book of World Records. In addition to being tall, he bore an uncanny resemblance to Abraham Lincoln—a fact he embellished every year for President's Day. Every kid thought it was cool when he'd dress up in a black suit, long coat, and top hat. It was the '70s, so his bearded chops were semi in style. But the most unique memory I have of Mr. Stone involved a fire drill.

Leading up to the day, Mr. Stone and our teachers had been talking with us about how this fire drill would be different. Apparently, the county fire chief and a large part of the department would be on hand to observe. I supposed they would time or at least monitor our exit from the building. Every day of the week there was some sort of activity or reminder of the upcoming drill. Finally, the day arrived.

From our classroom window we saw the big red fire truck pull into place. We half hoped to see a dalmatian appear, but instead we saw another red truck pull in, and then another. When the driver emerged, we saw a clean crisp, white dress shirt and tie. Everything about him was official; this guy had to be the fire chief we'd heard about all week. With all the officials present and in place, the alarm was sounded, and the drill began.

Like every drill before, we got up from our seats and formed an orderly line. The buzzing of the alarm and flashing emergency light fixtures, we'd all seen before. However, as we made our way down the hall there were things we'd not seen. The first was when we saw firemen in place monitoring our exit. We passed them and made our way down the hall. On one wall was a big sign on bright yellow paper, lines depicted flames and one word, fire! These were new and made things scarier, even for fifth graders. We figured we were safe as we made it to the stairs. Then on the landing of the staircase, we saw another huge sign. This one depicted a smoky scene and another one-word message, duck! Unfortunately, this one-word message would be our undoing.

No one would admit to being first, but someone quacked and then another. A teacher attempted to stop the behavior, but it was too late. The rest of us joined in. Some of us even tucked our arms like wings and began to waddle. I might have been the first. We, the fifth grade, chose this moment to quack and waddle our way to safety. The other grades were safe outside and behaving. They became our audience and appeared to appreciate our performance. Some giggled and a few others joined in.

Teachers moved to regain control of their ducklings—I mean students. I knew we'd crossed a line when Mr. Stone placed his head in his hands. Maybe he and the fire chief were trying to hide smiles. But it was no laughing matter when Mr. Stone gathered us all up to express his disappointment in our behavior.

● ● ●

When was the last time you got caught misbehaving? I'm not necessarily talking about when we were kids. I know I've been pulled over and ticketed for speeding. On more than one occasion I've cut someone off in traffic. Have you ever pretended to be something or someone you're not? Maybe you've embellished a resume to get a job, or maybe it's something else. Whether it was good fun or something more serious, there is good news. God has a history of using the very circumstances that left us broken. Like a potter or sculptor, He transforms them into incredible works of art.

The same things you think have destroyed you, might be exactly what qualifies you as an expert. Maybe the mess you are in is not a drill. Just because you think there is no clear path out of your fire does not mean you are disqualified. You know you've heard it. The calm voice inside just keeps calling your name. He's there with open arms, like the father of the prodigal son. Maybe you've run away or tried to run away from your past. Your money, your spouse, or so-called friends are long gone. The party is over.

You've been "sleeping in your barn" and "eating with your pigs" for far too long. Go home—your Father, our Father, is waiting to surround you with His arms, fill you with love, dress you, feed you, and make you anew.

● ● ●

There were many things I learned to not do during the county-wide fire drill. But from elementary school I also carried with me some great friends and experiences. One of which was our time in the music room. I was the kid who—at least musically speaking—was caught up in everything. My Babci always got us to watch the Lawrence Welk Show. It was music from her era. A big band with Mr. Welk as the bandleader. The show had a cast of pretty girls with big hair and bigger gowns. Every guy could dance and sing and seemed to wear powder-blue or white tuxedos on most episodes. After each skit or performance, the camera would cut back to the show's maestro, who would typically react with a sincere "Wasn't that a-wonderful?"

The show was certainly not what most kids would choose to watch. Times were different then. Granted we probably watched because Babci was so good about providing us with the snacks our parents did not allow. Add to the mix they only had one television. Any kid will tell you, watching TV beats no TV. But the primary reason I watched her show was because she'd join us to watch ours. Sha-Na-Na was another music variety show featuring the do-wop group Sha-Na-Na, who dressed as and parodied 1950s street culture. The skits and musical guests were based in the '50s. The fact that Babci not only watched but sang and danced with our show stood out to me. Maybe because she showed appreciation for a show in sharp contrast to hers, I figured I'd better find something to appreciate in different types of music. And something changed when I heard songs from the Sugar Hill Gang and the Fat Boys.

There in the basement of her house I'd sit and listen to her off-white, plastic, tabletop transistor radio. It had the manual adjusting knob and gold-colored metal rods. I suppose they helped capture the radio waves and put them in the speaker. Regardless of how it worked, I was hooked on this new music. It was way different from the Lawrence Welk Show and the Big Band sounds she helped me appreciate. Rap was even different than the rock and roll and disco of the '70s. Eventually Christian music even had its own rap music category. I still didn't know everything about Jesus, but something told me He'd be cool with a funky flow.

My first taste of Christian rap was the group DC Talk, I'd hear them at a Fellowship of Christian Athletes camp a year or two later. For some reason only two of the three members were there. My mind was fully engaged in trying to grasp the lyrics with their sound. I didn't rap yet, but the kids in my group knew I could beatbox. Beatboxing is creating a drumbeat rhythm and percussion sounds using only your mouth and a microphone. There is a lot of spittle involved. I was nowhere as good as the sounds the Fat Boys could make. But when the DC Talk guy asked the group if anyone could make the sound, my friends pointed to me. It was the first of two times I would beatbox with DC Talk. I am quite sure they wouldn't remember, but it was etched in my brain. For a time, I thought I would be the Marky Mark of Christian rap music. I even wrote and recorded a few songs and performed at local churches under the name Kevy-Kev. I know, not exactly original.

A few years later I went to college. I can still remember standing in the Olive Branch bookstore in Clarion, Pennsylvania. This place would let you listen to music before you purchased it. To place this on a historical musical timeline, it was well past 45s and 8-tracks, just before CDs, and decades before electronic MP3s and downloads. These were the golden days of cassettes, making mixtapes, and sometimes having to rewind with a pencil eraser. In the bookstore, I was previewing the latest tape from a new group called SFC (Soldiers for Christ). The sounds coming through the headphones took me back to those first moments in my grandmother's basement. After purchasing the tape, I discovered a song entitled "Mr. Brain," which really engaged me:

> *I label religion, which is a manmade structure or division*
> *of reaching God,*
> *But there, slipp'n or in other words miss'n the truth!*
> *Because religion is phony, it's like generic bologna,*
> *...*
> *It's noth'n but bunch of massive of confusion.*
> *People think they winnin' but they really are losin'.*
> *Some speak this, and some speak that, but really what*
> *they speak'n ain't based on fact.*[2]

I would love to go on but think I'd better stop there as I believe I've caused my poor Polish grandmother to roll over in her grave. Allow me to explain what I think the lyrics mean.

First, I acknowledge religions themselves can be helpful. I can see us, the creation, attempting to grasp the concept of a loving God. I can see where rituals, religious practices, regular meetings, and avid study of scripture can all work toward our human attempts to understand and make sense of a triune God. I have great respect for those who have devoted their lives to the study, interpretation, and sharing of the collection of books known worldwide as the Bible.

In my own limited study, I can see where Christian, Jewish, Islamic, and several other of the world's religions strive to help us make sense of the unseen. I see within Christianity that the denominations share some key common ground. My point is not to start another religious debate: I think we can all agree our history is full of best intentions gone astray.

Not to be confused with a certain rock band, but have you ever heard the saying "Keep It Simple, Stupid"? It's one I've heard in a variety of settings. One of my coaches would yell this out as

[2] "Mr. Brain," songwriter Chris Cooper, 1989.

a reminder to simply do our job and block the right guy. I would hear this again while training in a variety of customer service jobs. It is also a common marketing technique. In general, it points out how all too often we humans have the tendency to over-complicate things. Perhaps it's some attempt to validate a strongly held opinion.

Again, it is not my intention to wreck someone's house of cards or be overly simplistic. I mean, after all ... when we are talking about a triune God, an ultimate Creator who is omnipresent, before, after and throughout time, whose past—as in the person of Jesus, born of a virgin, marking a change in recorded history from BC to AD, escaping death as infant, largely being unrecorded as a teenager, starting a ministry at thirty questioning the practices of the day—is present still, to this day as the Holy Spirit, despite only indirectly having access to TV, radio, or social media. Oh, and this concept where the Spirit remains here, with us, until He comes back? I mean, seriously, what could be complicated about that? (Sarcasm intended.)

Only in the Christian world, with those recognizing a triune God that I attempted to represent above, can we hope to keep it simple. I know it's impossible for us humans to fully grasp the concept of just the first part, the Alpha and Omega. Some of us can easily get hung up and tune out right there. And on the other side this concept of Holy Spirit or Holy Ghost, who is available to us here and now, this too, can be a bit out there.

But what might happen if we just look at the middle section, when Christ was here living among us? I think most of us, even nonbelievers, acknowledge that Jesus was a real, historical person. Is it too simplistic to look at the words He spoke as recorded in books Christian believers acknowledge?

Picture the scene. First, the religious believers who were totally engaged, seeking to learn more, and show others the way to God in their religion. They formed the question and asked this thirty-something teacher, "All right, Mr. Smartypants Prophet, which of the commandments is the greatest, the most important?"

Isn't it just like us humans to be seeking a shortcut or the ultimate black-and-white answer? The response is well documented: Love the Lord your God with all your heart, soul, and mind. That's the first. Next is very similar: love your neighbor the same way you love yourself. Everything else hangs on the first two.

On one hand, maybe the response is a rationalization for all the religious and denominational tensions that remain even today. But on the other hand, I don't think it could've been much more clearly presented. Could the answer we all too easily complicate and dress up with our own rules and expectations actually be so simple, so honest, so pure, and yet (if we are honest) so hard?

When I sit with this question, I think I understand what the rich young prince felt when he was told to sell off what he had. Too often we prefer to cling to what we know, what is familiar. When Jesus responded to doubting Thomas in that upper room. He told him to go ahead, press in, push deeper into the wounds so you know it's really me. While I think traditions and familiarity are all well and good, I think the same invitation given to Thomas is extended to us in the here and now.

● ● ●

Are you being beckoned to deeper waters? Are you afraid to go deeper? Maybe it's similar to when we were little kids and we didn't want to walk deeper into the pool, the lake, or the ocean. Granted, the moments when a wave comes, you have to suddenly draw in a breath, go under, and hope your foot reaches a solid bottom in order to push yourself back above the waterline … those can be scary! Or even those moments when you are swimming freely you might wonder, Is there something swimming with me? Are my arms and legs strong enough to keep going? Did I wait the required thirty minutes my grandmother told me about to avoid a cramp?

Or maybe you were like me when you were in a swimming

pool. Maybe you played the game to see how long you could hold your breath. My sisters and I would see how many times we could dart back and forth from one end of the pool to the other, with just a single breath. At first you are swimming along smoothly, through the chlorine—or the challenges of life. We can see the goal, the other end of the pool. Maybe we've gotten really good at this game of holding our breath and developed an ability to persevere. Maybe we keep going despite the challenges we face and the growing ache we start to feel in our lungs. Maybe like me, you would do nearly anything to beat or outshine your friends or older sibling by going a little further than they could. Even when it meant the ache, the need for fresh air in your lungs, became a burning.

I'll admit to more than one time holding my breath a little too long. Coming up gasping for air or coughing out water. I was a bit too competitive. And maybe—like my stubbornness to win the swimming game—we also have the desire to be right. What happens if we keep it simple and breathe in the fresh air ... which is always there. Are you being called a little deeper? Is it time to duck under and swim freely? We need to remember it doesn't matter if we are trying to survive a fire drill, win a swimming game, or figure out if God really loves us. Rest assured the fresh air of a relationship with Jesus' love is always accessible and more life-giving than any rules.

CHAPTER 11

More Than Enough

Her name was Whitney. Her brunette hair made her the prettiest girl in the entire school. Fortunately, our last names were alphabetically close, so my locker ended up right beneath hers. We got to talk and exchange looks. When she sprained an ankle and had to use crutches, I volunteered to carry her books to her locker each morning. Unfortunately, her last name was the same as our school principal. She was his daughter.

It was time for a school dance, and these were new to us. They had everything you'd expect to see at any junior high dance. Lights pulsed in rhythm with the music and cut through the haze from the fog machine. Rays of light from a mirrored ball cast their beam over bleachers and their spell over us. Teachers and administrators were chaperones. They spent the evening making sure none of the "seriously dating" couples did anything too frisky. The rest of us were wallflowers on opposite sides of the gym. Occasionally, we met in the middle when a popular song was played. After three or four upbeat songs, the slowed-down rhythms of a love song came on. The couples would either move to the dance floor from their make-out corners or stay out if they had been dancing with us. But the beginning of a slow song sent most retreating to our predesignated spots—the rare exception being the occasional guy having the nerve to ask a girl he liked to dance. After watching and participating in the ebb and flow of dancing and retreating, I decided to take my chance.

Maybe it was the darkness of the gym, perhaps it was her pretty dark brown hair, her nice smile, or the nice things she would say to me as we met at our lockers. The fast song ended and one about rain the shade of purple started to play. I didn't know if she'd say yes, but if she did, I knew I'd have a solid eight minutes to impress her and, just maybe, win her heart. I approached her and the surrounding group of friends. I am sure my knees were knocking. My heart was racing, and my palms were getting a bit moist with nervousness. I asked if she'd like to dance. She smiled and said, "Sure." Her friends giggled as they walked away.

We stood in the awkward first dance pose. My hands on her hips and her hands safely on my shoulders. Any chaperone, even her dad, would've approved of the space between us. During the first dance, there is only so much two kids can talk about. I think eventually we ran out of things to say or just decided to stop talking. Maybe we were getting tired of dancing but eventually her hands moved from my shoulders and clasped just behind my head. Likewise, I moved my hands together, making sure to not touch her butt. After all, this was just a first dance. Despite the respectable distance between us, I was certain that had I made any wrong move, her dad would pounce on me from out of the shadows.

The song ended and a few days after the dance, my heart broke. I learned she'd started to "go with" a boy who nicknamed her Certs. My budding Romeo ego was in disbelief. I'd been friendly, nice, even carried her books—and she goes for a guy who nicknamed her after a candy you take when your breath stinks? Clearly, I had a lot to learn about junior high love.

•   •   •

A few months later I watched this newfangled sport called soccer. Mom thought it would be a great sport for me to try. I'd only seen one soccer game on TV. The best player on one of the teams had an Afro. It was especially huge and, I thought, incredibly cool. I negotiated with my mom: if I could get my hair that big, I would try soccer.

I should've suspected something was up when Mom announced she'd made an appointment with her hairdresser. I thought "A hairdresser! Why not a barber?" I panicked and began to wonder exactly what I had agreed to. The appointment day came, and we were in some lady's basement. I didn't mind the wash and shampoo but the pungent smell, what was that? I thought something had died. The next thing I knew she was rolling my hair in tight little rollers. I listened, as she and my mom talked for what seemed like hours. There was something they said that caught my attention, the word permanent. But the only thing I knew about that word related to those black markers. Eventually she finished binding my hair in the roller things. She adjusted my chair to place me under the dome-shaped dryer. I saw myself in the mirror and I was mortified.

The rollers were the same pink shade I'd seen my mom use on my grandmother's hair. I thought I was going to die and was now at least grateful to be secure in a basement. This eliminated the chance my friends would see me. When the appointment ended the rollers were out and my hair was enormous. The lady even gave me a cool black pick; it folded up with one green handle and one red. It could barely fit in my back pocket. She told me how to use it. I thought it was awesome! My hair was as big as the guys who danced on Soul Train. I thought it looked so cool. This was not the same opinion as one of the girls on my bus.

It started on the morning bus ride, with a girl who'd gotten on before me. Her smirky face and tone kept commenting and asking why my hair was so big and poofy. I tried to play it off like no big deal, but she kept at it. I told her it was an Afro or 'fro for short, as if to point out only the cool people would shorten a four-letter word to just three. I produced the pick from my back pocket and showed how I now had to do my hair. She wouldn't stop. Eventually we made it to school, and I hoped the incident was over. But she picked right back up on the ride home, on bus number eighty-one.

Mr. Kidd was the driver. He was a no-nonsense older gentleman. He drove the bus and seemed to have his eyes on the rearview mirror, at least as much, if not more than, the road. The mirror allowed him to watch his passengers' behavior. He could easily and frequently be heard above the noise of the bus and the kids. He'd holler out someone's name followed by "You'd better sit down" or "Turn 'round and zip it!"

His ultimate threat was turning us into "the man." We naturally assumed he meant either one of our male principals. Our head principal was the dad of the prettiest brunette. For obvious reasons, I didn't want to be turned into the principal, as this would surely blow any future chance I had with his daughter. The assistant principal, Mr. Trumbower, was worse. He was an enormously tall individual and easy to spot, even next to the much older and taller eighth graders.

Despite my reservations about being sent to the man, the onslaught from this girl regarding my hair was quickly escalating. When she asked me my name I replied, "Kevin." She said, "See, even your name sounds like a girl's name." It was true; Kevin was not a common name in the '70s. But it didn't seem girly to me. She wasn't impressed when I mentioned the only other person I knew with the same name was also a boy. She kept at it. I panicked. In the morning, I had explained my hair was like the guy playing soccer.

I'd already produced the pick and even did my best to be as cool as the guys on TV. Now in the afternoon she was questioning my gender?

She was saying my name was a girl's name and even added an a to make it Kev-vina. Had she seen me in the hairdresser's chair? I sure hope Mom hadn't taken and shared a picture of me in pink rollers. I was pressed at all sides. When she again said I was a girl, I felt I had no choice. I stood, unzipped my pants, pulled down my underwear, and proclaimed, "There, how many girls you know have one of those?"

I did not think Mr. Kidd would be glancing up in his mirror at the exact same time. His mouth was open as if to say he'd never seen this happen during all his years driving bus eighty-one, not ever! He called my name and told me to sit in the seat behind his. We made it to the bus stop in front of my house. I was sure he was going to walk me to the front door and tell my parents about the whole thing. But he didn't, instead he pulled out his pad of bus behavior reports. I didn't even know such a thing existed, but he completed the form and handed my copy to me.

He simply said, "Tomorrow morning, 'stead of going to the auditorium, you need to go see the man."

Technically, he did not instruct me to show my parents, so I didn't. I didn't get a lot of sleep because of his last two words. Oddly enough, when I reported to the office the next morning, there was no man. Just the secretary and Ms. Assid, the other assistant principal. The secretary asked why I was there. I handed her my copy of the bus behavior report. I was ashamed and looking down at the ground. I couldn't see if she laughed when she read it, but she soon disappeared. When she came back, she directed me to a chair and said Ms. Assid would be right with me.

I thought, A lady? The lady assistant principal? As much as I was afraid of the principal and Mr. Trumbower, I thought I at least had a shot with them. Only a guy could understand how a full-on assault of your manliness might warrant a flashing of your manhood. But now I had to talk to a woman? I found myself suddenly wishing Mr. Kidd had walked me to the door and told my parents. The spanking would've been far less painful and embarrassing than talking with Ms. Assid.

Eventually she came out and called me into her office. I sat down as she asked me to explain what happened. I recounted the morning events: how the girl went on and on, how I hadn't responded, how I hoped the situation was over as we'd arrived to school. I told Ms. Assid how the girl was wrong, how her words and accusations continued the entire ride home. I told her in detail everything I had done attempting to prove to the girl on the bus I wasn't a girl. I couldn't look at her when I told her about my not-so-grand declaration.

Even though her name was pronounced the exact same way as the dangerous, corrosive liquid our science teacher talked about, Ms. Assid was very kind and surprisingly understanding. While she obviously didn't condone my behavior and made me promise the incident would not repeat itself, she went the next step. She told me if something like this happened again, I had other options. She let me know I could come tell her. I left the office confused but encouraged. As fearful as I was when Mr. Kidd wrote the report, as much as I had hyped up the meeting with the man, and as certain as I was that the meeting would not end well, it seemingly had. And I think this is how it is with God.

●　　●　　●

It's easy for us to be overwhelmed with the challenges we face in life. They come with hard names: addiction, lost job, cancer, death of a child, or a spouse who unexpectedly walks out. Feel free to insert the most recent thing you've faced. The big ones sure seem to make the lesser ones—running late, a flat tire, or a common cold—all the more unbearable. Jesus knew about all of these. He knew the good, the bad, and especially the uncomfortable. He lived it. He chose to come down and be among us. And He chooses to pursue us every day.

They say Jesus was equal parts man and divine. And maybe that's why He gets us. We know He was presented with our "people problems" daily. Like the time His disciples wanted to dismiss the crowd. Jesus had preached all day and the disciples wanted to send the people off to get their own food. The disciples weren't being unfaithful, disobedient, or sinful, they were just being practical and human. They thought they didn't have the resources to provide food for so many. But Jesus saw an opportunity to show them, and show us, we have access to far more than we know. He is the God of more than enough. Even enough to fill twelve baskets with leftovers.

He understands daily demands and wants us to come to Him daily. He knows this life can leave us feeling like the dog under the table just waiting for a scrap to fall. But Jesus is patiently waiting, beckoning us out from under the table. He is inviting us to sit next to Him at the table. Just like the king who sent his servants out to invite the commoners to his party. Just like the father of the prodigal son who waited and watched for his son every day, Jesus is waiting for us. He longs for our return so He can clothe us in forgiveness and throw us a feast fit for a king. There is no experience necessary. He loves you just the way you are. You are enough.

Maybe like me, you aren't accustomed to this kind of love. Maybe you've experienced a failed marriage, or two, or three. Maybe you didn't know your parents, maybe they put you up for adoption. Despite loving adoptive parents, there is still a small hole (or gaping wound) left by parents who weren't ready. Maybe you sit beside the grave of a dear friend, a parent, a sibling, or a child. Grief and sorrow take time to process. I'm not saying it's easy. But I wonder are you, are we, still choosing to live in a grave of our own making?

Just like Lazarus, you are the one Jesus loves. You are the one He is calling out of your self-imposed grave. Jesus has already done the work. All you need to do is respond. He is calling your name. Stand up, walk out of the grave. He will send whomever He needs to help remove your burial clothes. He wants to envelop you and clothe you with His gleaming robe of dignity and grace. He longs to place a ring on your finger and a crown on your head. He sees you as more valuable than proving your identity on a bus ride. He says you are more innocent than the first dance of two junior high students. You are more handsome or beautiful than the principal's child, even if she is a brunette. You are His, a son or daughter of a God bigger than any Afro. Together, the Father, Son, and Holy Spirit are right now providing endless love. Open your hands and receive.

If you still doubt God could love you this much it's OK, I did too. For years, I camped out. I lingered far too long around the metaphorical monuments I built to my hurts. I masked it, dressed it up in an attempt to cover the shame. I spent years looking to other people and things for validation. The reality I now know is what I said before: Jesus has done the work. You don't need to prove who you are to the girl on the bus. You don't need a cool hairstyle and a pick. You don't even need to date the principal's daughter. He loves you just the way you are.

CHAPTER 12

The Voice of the Shepherd

My sophomore year of high school was a new beginning. I say that because my freshman year I was known by one of two names: I was either the younger brother of the senior on the girls' basketball team or Pizza Face. It sounds harsh, but it's what my wrestling teammates called me. The name accurately reflected the impact of acne combined with bumps and bruises from practice. I'd investigated all the school groups but hadn't found a niche outside of sports. I wasn't into smoking, so I didn't fit in with the "heads" who had to get a signed parent permission slip to be on the smoking block. Which, by the way, was located right next to the cardboard dumpster. Am I the only one who finds that questionable? I couldn't sing or act, so there were no high school musical choir or drama roles for me. I struggled with the English language, let alone foreign languages, so the cool clubs like Latin,

Spanish, and French were out. I got along with most everybody but was not super popular, so winning student council elections was not in the cards for me. After my thorough search, I jumped into Fellowship of Christian Athletes primarily because my wrestling coaches ran it.

I'd been going to church and getting something out of it, although I couldn't exactly quantify it for you. It was a challenge because our church was on the opposite side of town from where we lived. None of my friends from school or sports attended our church, which means I ended up with church friends and school friends. It was awkward but I managed. While I had a vague understanding of denominational differences, I had at least heard of God, and I was an athlete. So when Coach Trent invited me to consider joining the group and attending the weekend, I was all in. I mentioned it to my parents, and maybe because it was a religious activity, they thought it was a good idea. They signed the paper and paid the fee.

Anybody who has ever attended one knows what a Weekend of Champions is all about. If you don't know, allow me to briefly explain. It's a weekend during which primarily athletes—but really anyone in their school's Fellowship of Christian Athletes chapter—goes on a retreat of sorts. The biggest part of the weekend was a chance for each of us to take a deeper dive and learn a little more about our concept of God.

Eventually the day came for all of us to load up onto the school bus; nearly all the boys and girls of our chapter were attending. Some were already "dating" each other, some wanted to be dating, and some were scared and clueless, like me. As the wheels of the bus rumbled over the miles of asphalt, I wondered what this weekend would hold. Coach had mentioned a few selling points when inviting me to attend: there would be athletic competitions, food, and some talks. He had me at competitions and food.

• • •

As we arrived at the 4-H center on Smith Mountain Lake, the first thing I saw was the putt-putt golf course. I wasn't a golfer, but golf is a connection with my dad and the memories of early summer mornings he'd take me golfing. He'd let me tee it up from the 150-yard markers at the Blue Hills Golf Course. I think I may still hold the record for lost balls. I was never anywhere close to consistent—but as they say, even a blind squirrel finds a nut every once in a while. And sure enough, every now and then, I'd "hold the club with the right grip," "not over swing," "let the club do the work," and "keep my head down." These were just some of the things my dad endlessly suggested, and he was right. When I did these things, I'd connect with a great shot.

That miniature golf course at the 4-H center took me back to a time on the first green with my dad. We'd both made it to the green—he'd made it in regulation, and I may have been in double digits. I think I was putting downhill from about six feet away. Dad pulled the flag and walked it back like the pros on TV. He was making his "paintbrush suggestion," telling me where to hit the ball so it would roll into the cup. I must've looked up or stubbed the club. The ball whizzed past the first hole at what seemed like Mach 4 and kept rolling. Some public courses have two separate hole placements on their greens. Mine managed to keep moving, rolling and turning and eventually trickling into the wrong hole with the kerplunkitty-plunk plink every golfer loves to hear. I remember Dad raising his hand, dropping the flag, and celebrating as though I had just won a green jacket at the Masters. Even if it went in the wrong hole sixty-five feet away, Dad said it was good.

I think this is the way God sees us when we give our best attempts at love, justice, feeding the hungry, clothing the naked, welcoming the homeless. He's not concerned with did we anticipate the undulation of the green or which club we used. Kind of like my dad, our heavenly Father isn't even worried if we get it in the right hole. He says it right there, love God and love others. Seek Him first and everything else gets sorted out later.

•   •   •

We passed the putt-putt course, and I was a little surprised to see buses from surrounding school districts. I'd forgotten Coach had mentioned other kids from other schools would be there. My numbers could be off, but I'd estimate attendance was typically between seventy-five and one hundred kids for the weekend. We would all be divided into different groups, each with a college-aged or adult leader. The first year I was anxious about being randomly mixed into teams with people I didn't know. Maybe, like me, you aren't too good at remembering new names and faces. But eventually I saw it for what it was: a way to immediately move us out of our comfort zones and open us to discovering new friends and aspects of this thing called faith.

Eventually we got settled into our concrete cabins. We'd been separated by gender and, of course, a small army of male and female adult chaperones. Then we gathered in the cafeteria/auditorium for the first meal. I can't remember exactly what it was but in the three years I attended, I don't recall ever going hungry.

I can remember the music striking up. The strumming sound of acoustic guitars made me remember Sunday mornings and the talented musicians at our church. There were funny sing-a-longs, skits, and talks designed to help young athletes connect the dots between our athleticism and faith. Maybe there was more to our sports than just winning and losing. One year we even had a special group of musicians coming to provide some cutting-edge music which was more my thing at the time.

Teachers didn't talk about ADHD when I was younger. But if they had, I am sure I could've been a poster child. The indicators showed up on my report cards as teacher comments like "needs to sit still," "easily distracted," and "struggles with new concepts" seemed to repeat like a skipping record. But this wasn't the case with every class. There were topics that interested me and teachers who just had a knack for pulling me in. Gym class and sports were two things that garnered my full attention. I think this is at least part of the reason I enjoyed football and wrestling. The idea of formulating a plan of attack or drawing up a play and having to adjust on the fly based upon the reaction or inaction of the opponent—that kept me engaged. This Weekend of Champions held my attention but in an entirely different way. Yes, there were tugs-of-war and all sorts of fun, but in the stillness, in the more reflective moments, there was a calm, inviting me to probe deeper. Maybe like Jesus invited Thomas when they were together in the upper room. I'd heard my Protestant friends talk about being "born again." While I sure as heck didn't understand the concept, there was something at work. It slowly built up to our last morning. It was after another delicious breakfast.

I was outside, in front of the meeting hall by the flagpole. The hall was perched atop a gentle slope that led down to the waters of Smith Mountain Lake. Over the weekend my group of guys would meet by the pole to go to activities, to eat, or sometimes just to reflect and pray. I can remember walking right past the flagpole. I had started to walk toward the parking lot, and was maybe four or five steps beyond the pole when I audibly heard a voice call out, "Hey Kevin." My ears recognized the voice. It felt and sounded familiar, but I couldn't put a face to the voice. Was it my group leader or a member of my team? I just couldn't place it.

As I started to turn in response, I had time to think about who might be speaking to me. I thought for sure I would see my leader—or maybe it was my coach. While I didn't quite have the image in my brain, it was a calming presence, and I knew I was safe. I was a little startled as I completed my turn but found no one was there. No group leader, no coach, no random kid playing tricks, or pretty girl feigning a deep male voice. I started to think I had imagined it but at the same time I knew I hadn't. I did hear the voice. I looked around to double-check no one was pranking me. Maybe Coach Trent had upped his practical-joke game. But no one was there.

After standing there and thoroughly scanning the area, I determined there was no one around, at least no human presence. In my mind I replayed the sketch from the night before about alerting each other for bears, but there were no bears either. I started to retrace my steps and approached the pole. I still half expected a friend, teammate, or someone to jump out and surprise me. I carefully walked past the poll and approached the worn wooden split rail fence—placed there, I am sure, to prevent kids like me from needlessly accelerating down the slope.

I got to the fence when something came over and warmed me. I couldn't tell you if it was from the inside out or the outside in. It was more loving than a mother's hug and more filling than any of the meals we'd eaten. All I could see were kids my age. Some were laughing and enjoying themselves. Some were tossing Frisbees, others made their way to the basketball pavilion, and some were down by the lake just sitting and enjoying the majestic view. We weren't divided by sport, age, size, race, gender, denomination, or school affiliation. We were all there united in a purpose of playful fun, being together, investigating and pressing in. I don't know if it was the voice talking to me again or maybe just a thought came to mind: maybe this is what heaven could be like.

I suppose someone could go back and research the date and weather. Maybe it was just warm sunshine hitting my skin. Maybe it was a culmination of the Kumbaya events of the weekend. I am not saying the voice I heard was for sure God or even an angel. There was no glowing aura, no harp music, and no floating feathers. But I am at least open to any of those as possibilities to grasp what I was experiencing.

●　　●　　●

All these decades later, I still hear the calm voice. At least I can when I force myself away from the numerous daily obligations of being an adult, a small-business owner, and a ninja/gymnastics coach. I can hear it when I am able to sing in the choir and when the lyrics we sing jump off the page and hit my heart.

Maybe you've had a moment when the words you hear, read, or sing cause you to stop. Maybe you felt the frog well up in your throat, a sudden inexpressible joy, or maybe just enough of your defenses came down, allowing a tear to form and fall as you tried to conceive the amount of love He has for you. Maybe, just maybe, that morning on the hilltop it was our Father throwing down a little manna to provide a small glimpse of what the end of our journey might look like.

God will do this from time to time. God is not limited. At times He is soft or warm like the weekend at the lake. At other times God is blunt and more direct. We are told this life won't be easy, and that we will have our share of troubles. Some of them will be small and more easily managed. Some of them may even allow us to think we can handle it on our own. But then come the bigger, more challenging waves, each with its own name. Cancer, death, mass shootings, and September 11, just to name a few. Maybe you are like me and are tempted to take it on—solo. But life in this world has a way of showing us how we are far better off when we are anchored in fellowship.

Paul was one of Jesus' friends, and he started a church in Greece and wrote them letters to encourage them. In one of his letters, he reminded them, "God is faithful, who has called you into fellowship with His Son, Jesus Christ our Lord." Who called you? Was it your parents, a coach, maybe a friend or pastor or someone else? They may have been the body but I'm asking us to consider who was the spirit? If we are honest with ourselves, as humans we are each going to mess it up. It doesn't matter if we putted the ball into the wrong hole, took the wrong job, married the wrong person, or heard the wrong diagnosis. There's a book in the Bible called Psalms. It's written by a few different writers and some people think of them as love letters from God. One of them assures us, "The Lord is near to the brokenhearted and saves the crushed in spirit." His Spirit is even closer than a friend. He left it for each of us and in each of us. We have access.

In a second letter, Paul wrote to his friends, "But we hold this treasure in earthen vessels, that the surpassing power may be of God and not from us." God poured Himself into us and just like the sheep hear the voice of their shepherd, we, too, hear the Spirit when He calls each of us. When those bigger waves reach the shores of our lives, there will be a lot of noise distracting and maybe even preventing us from hearing. Fortunately, God is bigger than any wave. Let's tune in and hear it fresh in our hearts again: "The Lord is near to the brokenhearted and saves the crushed in spirit." Here in the crushing times, He's whispering, "Can you trust me this much?"

CHAPTER 13

The Rescue

I had a friend named Larry. We grew up together, watched the same TV shows, went to the same schools, played the same sports, and occasionally liked the same girls. We talked about everything. Frequently he'd shout out, "Jesus, Mary, and Joseph!" The intensity of his words betrayed his stated intentions. He'd tell you he was asking them to intercede or asking for their help. As someone who heard him more than once, I can tell you it sure sounded more like he was cussing. As kids, we paid attention to the characters of the Christmas story. Let's face facts: Mary and Jesus shine the brightest. You can't help but be drawn in by her story and the birth in a manger. But they weren't alone. We wondered what happened to Mary's husband Joseph. He's built up in all the early scenes, where he learns about Mary being pregnant. We see where he contemplated quietly divorcing her, and where he's corrected back on course by the angel. He arranges transportation to the census. Once there, he secures the best available accommodations. Granted, it's not a brand-name hotel with free wi-fi or breakfast buffet. But it is a safe place for his wife and child.

But what we always found most interesting was how after Jesus was born, Joseph faded into the background. Here was God's earthly father, a guy who, by all accounts, had been through a lot, wrestled with some big challenges, and done quite a bit for his wife and their child. Imagine the parent-child relationship between Jesus, Mary, and Joseph. I wonder if, like a lot of dads (OK, I wonder if like me), Joseph more times than not found himself with his foot in his mouth.

I can't help but think Joseph had to feel like a third wheel. Like the evening after they found Jesus preaching in the temple. Do you think Joseph lay in bed that night and somewhere in the silence of his thoughts, he wondered, God, I'm married to Mary, the woman you chose above all others to give birth to your perfect, sinless Son. And Jesus, clearly there is something about Him. He is wise beyond His years. And then there's me. Joseph, a simple carpenter. Exactly what do I bring to the table?

And why is it that soon after the temple event, we don't hear about Joseph ever again? We are all left to wonder. Clearly more than once Joseph had doubts even though he was chosen. On both his best and worst days, He too needed a rescue. If there were some odd dynamics and doubts in Jesus's family, should we be surprised when some of those same things happen in our own? We often hear about idyllic parent-child relationships. Larry and I grew up and saw this portrayed on television. We had role models like the Ingalls family on Little House on the Prairie. Every challenge was resolved in a single episode. The Waltons always ended the same way. The camera would take in a view of the house. Panning upwards, it floated above the house like an angel. The voices of Ma and Pa, each of the kids, and grandma and grandpa could be heard sweetly saying good night, as crickets quietly chirped, a few bells and harmonica notes were softly played. The sounds combined and lifted to heaven like a prayer each night. While those TV shows are enjoyable, we know the questions Joseph likely asked, because we ask them ourselves. We know all too well how real life often requires more than a sixty-minute episode with a tidy roll of credits to play itself out.

●　　●　　●

Like the kids on The Waltons, I love my momma, but this didn't mean she and I didn't occasionally butt heads. Especially during the blissfully ignorant days approaching my teens—you know, when teens and preteens have all the answers. I remember thinking I had my entire life mapped out. And this would lead to a great many interesting conversations and sometimes an argument with my mom.

Remember back when I said people change? Well, the same can be said for methods of disciplining children. This isn't badmouthing anyone. It's just how things were, and yes, there were plenty of times I made it clear I needed discipline. During my teens, dad sometimes quietly pointed out why he thought Mom and I occasionally bumped heads. He said it was because she and I were so much alike. Like any mom, she had high expectations. In addition to being a mother of three (eventually five) children, she'd taken on the role of "office person" for the business. I can remember way back to the first "office" in the house on Abbey Circle. It was on the basement level. It was the door on the left-hand side of the small hallway leading to my parents' bedroom. The office doubled as the laundry room and there was the desk Mom would sit at and quickly crunch numbers into the calculator. She was so fast it would make my head spin. Sometimes when she wasn't around, I would sneak into the office and randomly punch numbers and buttons, attempting to mimic her calculator proficiency.

It took a few years but eventually everything grew—their business and me too. They found a nicer, larger house for sale, which, like the Waltons,' was actually on a mountain. Chestnut Mountain, to be exact. I don't really recall the specifics as to why this larger house was available but somehow, someway, our family stood to have a very nice home. And guess who else lived on the mountain? Larry and his family. Not that we needed it, but the move afforded Larry and me more opportunity for mischief and adventure. The new house kept us in the same school system, so we moved to Deer Run Drive. Yes, on more than one occasion the neighborhood on a small mountain of the southern part of the Appalachian Mountains did occasionally have deer running down the street.

Spankings and discipline were packed up and continued in our new house. For parents who have never thought of spanking their child, trust me—back then, it was the norm. Spankings with hands, wooden spoons, and belts were not uncommon. If you happened to say something wrong or with a ring of sass, you could expect to quickly have a bar of soap jabbed in your mouth to literally wash it out.

For the most part, we were like most kids. We did our best to avoid trouble, but inevitably an innocent adventure would cross a mischievous line and get out of hand. When we were in trouble, we knew it! Getting spanked with my father's belt was something I did not ever forget. Perhaps this was by design. To be clear, I only got spanked with his belt one time. From then on, I knew I was pushing the limits when he would look at me and ask, "Do you want the belt?" I think this is when I also learned about rhetorical questions. Did he really think I would ever answer, "Oh yes, please"?

Now, if you know my dad, you know he is about the most non-confrontational human being on the planet. Even in the moments he tries to talk tough, the truth comes out. For example, he would give tours of the restaurant to any school group. He'd start by asking the group about what they wanted to study when they went to college. He'd get a host of answers and then ask the group, "What do you think I studied in school?" The typical answers were to be a chef or how to cook French fries. The older groups would even guess he'd studied business or entrepreneurship. He relished the opportunity to confuse and startle them when he'd refer to his training at the US Naval Academy and answer, "I was trained to be a killer!"

I am guessing the children—and likely more than one teacher—were somewhat stunned by his answer. Can't you just picture it? A group of fifteen to twenty first graders and a teacher standing in a large walk-in freezer, and "I was trained to be a killer" is the answer? Sounds like a scene straight out of a horror movie. Of course, he'd normally then go on to explain how you might go to school for one thing but end up doing something entirely different. Then one day he asked his questions, received their guesses, and gave his normal answer. But this day the group was standing in the freezer where all the hamburger patties were stored. And when he gave his "I'm a trained killer" answer—a small voice added, "of cows." My Dad does his very best to avoid arguments. But Larry's mom was different.

●　　●　　●

I think like a lot of moms, she was the enforcer at his house. More times than not I'd be over at his house and get to hear firsthand as she passionately spelled out all the things, she thought Larry did wrong. No, Larry wasn't perfect. None of us are. He did cause his fair share of trouble. On more than one occasion, he and

I both intercepted school progress reports, commonly known to us kids as "D/F slips." When we didn't, our moms got upset, took away TV time, designated a space for us to do our homework, or worse, threatened to remove us from our sports teams. And yes, occasionally we both got spanked. But as Larry got bigger, he told me he learned to defend himself. I didn't quite know what he meant and I wasn't sure I wanted to.

Larry and I didn't go to the same church. So, on Sunday afternoons after shooting hoops or playing video games, we'd occasionally compare notes from our Sunday mornings. But with siblings around at both of our houses we decided we had to build a secret place for ourselves. Over the years we spent countless hours in the woods constructing our fort. Every spare nail, scrap two-by-four and worn-out, wooden bike ramp was hauled into the woods and used to build our retreat. Our building techniques would not pass any OSHA or building codes. Our place wasn't insulated but it was a mostly weatherproof place for us to escape to. We even met there to hang out in the winter months. We'd meet and exaggerate the weather forecast and each make predictions on how much snow might fall. We always hoped school would be canceled. It was a safe place for us.

One Saturday Larry called me out of the blue and asked me to meet him at the fort. He didn't sound himself. He was serious and maybe even a little scared. He was already there when I arrived. Over the years we talked about God, sports, girls, and pretty much anything else. I knew there were tensions and I'd heard his mom get on his case, but on this trip, Larry let it all out.

He said, "It all started in the morning—she was upset about something she and I argued about last week. I thought it had blown over—one minute I was playing Atari and the next minute I was on the receiving end of her yelling and screaming." He went on and told me how he could feel the heat from her breath and even the spittle as her words spewed over him. He said, "She was all up in my face and said, 'Just who the hell do you think you are, you son-of-a bit—!'" He made it clear she finished the word, and continued, "She actually called me an SOB." I answered, "Oh my God! What did you say back?" He sheepishly answered, "I got in her face and said, 'Well, look who's calling the kettle black!'" Startled but admittedly happy for him, I said, "Good for you for standing up. What happened next?" He said, "For one second there was a look of total shock on her face and in the next her hand reared back to slap my face. She half hit my cheek but also caught my ear. The ringing sound was so intense I nearly fell to the floor."

Swallowing hard, I didn't know what else to say to my friend. It wasn't the first time he told me about his mom. He continued, "I wish she'd knocked me out and it had all ended. Instead, I jumped up and slapped her back." The last words spilled out as he started to cry. He said there was a flurry of other slaps, but his dad stepped in and separated them.

We spent much of the afternoon alone in our fort. Some words were spoken back and forth but even more conveyed silently. Our friendship grew even closer that day.

Thirty years passed. Larry and I were living on opposite sides of the country. But one of us was on a trip and we were able to grab a cup of coffee. In an instant it seemed we were back, safe in our fort. We meandered through topics like sports, our careers, and just life, but inevitably we came back to that day and the hard conversation. He said, "I'm not painting my mom in a bad light. Years of me working on me and piecing together the stories about her upbringing have helped me realize something. She was doing the best she could." I said, "Man you don't need to defend her. What happened was wrong. You don't need to say anything you don't want to."

He looked at me and with tears starting to well up in his eyes, he said, "I am still not proud of having slapped my mother. The grown-up version of me still does not like talking about it. But that was the last time Mom hit me." Those tears in his eyes were leaking out when he said, "There's still a little-kid version of me who occasionally thanks the almost-teenaged me for making it all stop." By this time, we both had sweaty eyes.

In the years since I've been an adult and a father, I've found myself in loud arguments with other adults. I've never hit anyone with my fists but the words I learned to defend or express myself were not helpful. I went through the process of unlearning those things. I still get help. I think we all need to spend some time and remind ourselves to constantly be relearning God's grace. It doesn't matter if we were the know-it-all teenager or, now, the busy parent. God is still working on you, me, and Larry. Let's embrace the idea and live like we know this truth—He's still working on each of us.

●   ●   ●

Unlike what we saw on The Waltons, I think sometimes real life has a way of revealing a simple truth to us. We are all flawed. Maybe like Joseph, we all have moments wondering, "Am I doing this right?"

There is a song I listen to frequently, called "Rescue." Now how a songwriter crafts their lyrics is an art form, truly a gift from God. For many of us, music allows us to hear God speaking. They are words of endless love, healing, and hope for us. They remind us of how big He is, that His foresight in how our fallen nature would leave us in need of far more than a fort with friends. God is able to see and speak through the space-time continuum.

Let's listen for His response: "I hear you whisper underneath your breath / I hear your SOS, your SOS."[3] We all need the Rescue—You, me, Larry, and Larry's mom too. He called me when she passed away. They never had the chance on this side of heaven to resolve or talk about the fight.

[3]"Rescue," songwriters Jason David Ingram, Lauren Daigle, Paul Brendon Mabury, lyrics © Centricity Music, 2018.

I don't think anyone likes to admit they need help, let alone an outright rescue. We all think we can figure things out on our own. Sometimes I think we have to be stronger and admit we really don't have all the answers.

And this is the wonderful part. It doesn't matter if you were brought up in a home with yelling and screaming or if your upbringing was more like the Waltons. It doesn't matter if you were born into a wealthy family or if your family started in a barn, like Jesus, Mary, and Joseph's. Our hope comes from knowing we can learn and grow into better versions of ourselves. For me and Larry, and maybe you too, here's where we are.

When I became a man, I put childish ways behind me. My truth is this, I am still right there, trying to put those ways behind me. Every day I am learning and working to discover what isn't working and simultaneously develop better ways. The world conspires to harden us, to reinforce the, "us against the world" thinking. It is hard but important work to grow up and still maintain our childlike faith. Maybe you are there too. And if so, it's OK!

Now we see but a poor reflection as in a mirror; then we shall see face to face. Now I know in part; then I shall know fully, even as I am fully known. And now these three remain; faith, hope and love.

What might happen if we spent time reminding ourselves—and the people who come into our lives—the simple things? No matter what we've been through in our past or where we find ourselves today. We can take heart because the rescue mission is, and has been, underway. It could be at night, or in the morning, but really any time is the right time to give ourselves these simple reminders.

Your Father loves you.

You are not alone.

And don't ever forget, He is working out the rescue.

CHAPTER 14

The Cage

In high school, I was an idiot. It's convenient to blame the surge of hormones and what seemed like every boy's desire. The guys I ran with wanted to have big muscles like the professional wrestlers or football players we watched on Saturday nights and Sunday afternoons. What seems silly now was normal then. At times we pictured ourselves as the "wrestling" heroes we'd watch on television. Our fantasy was enhanced by the fact our weight room was a caged corner of the locker room. In season, it's where we hung our stinky football pants, shoulder pads and helmets. They always left a pungent, but familiar smell only adolescent boys could grow to appreciate. Once the season was over, gear was stored, and weight equipment brought in. We'd head there every day for off-season workouts. We'd enter the cage and take turns living out the images we saw on TV.

When turned around, weight belts looked just like championship belts, minus the bling, of course. We all wanted to be one of pro-wrestling's Four Horsemen. We fancied ourselves as tough as those guys from Saturday night. We practiced our trash talking with a lisp like the American Dream, Dusty Rhodes. Two of us could pretend we were old school tag team champs, the brothers Ole and Arn Anderson. The feared Russian Bear, Nikita Koloff, was another favorite. He clobbered everyone with his finishing move, the "Russian sickle." We didn't seem to mind when we later found out Nikita was just a guy from Minnesota. There was a small part in each of us who wanted to be, the stylin', profilin', limousine-riding, jet flying, kiss-stealing, wheelin' dealin' son of a gun, Ric Flair, "WOOOooooooo." There was always someone new to emulate but every guy in our cage knew that "to be the man, you gotta beat the man."

We ran on teenage testosterone. We grew in height and muscle. Our mouths were constantly full of food, and in the cage, we were quite full of ourselves. We believed we were the undisputed, undefeated champions of the world. Or at least our school.

We were a band of brothers, but a bunch of knuckleheads. It was a blast and I think all of us have had this kind of moment. Maybe it wasn't an over-hyped caged workout, maybe it wasn't even in sports. Maybe for you it was in the classroom or on stage, in a play, blasting your instrument or vocal solo. Youth—dare I say life—should be full of these types of moments. I chased my peace in sports, looked for family in my teammates, and sought solace in lifting weights.

I was sort of crazy when it came to abdominals. I'd seen Sylvester Stallone do this in a Rocky movie. I'd climb upside down on the squat bar, hook my feet under the bar of the squat rack and hang down like Batman. From there I would do countless inverted sit-ups and even got to the point where I'd add resistance by holding some of the heavier plates. I was happy the day a coach saw me doing this. I finished a set and he said, "Lewis, you're nuts, you're crazy, you're like an animal." Sure, I guess the phrase could be taken either way, but in teenage boy lingo, it was high praise. Shortly after the workout, the coaches asked me to consider a change in position from running back to defensive line. In football, being on the line was called down in the trenches. It's where the big boys played and did the pushing and shoving. Testosterone helped me hear their suggestion as another compliment.

As big and muscular as I thought I was, I was barely five feet, ten inches tall and weighed one hundred fifty-five pounds— soaking wet with clothes on. The coaches said what I lacked in size I made up for in speed. Whether they really believed this or not, I don't know. But I didn't question them and bought in. I don't mean to overstate my working out, but from an early age it's where I felt at home—because I was in control. Like the other boys, I thought I was going to play in the NFL or maybe fight like the wrestlers on TV. Even if my dreams and aspirations weren't what others called normal, I told myself I could do it. You see, back when I was ten my parents gave me what I thought was the greatest gift ever, my very own weight bench. When I was lifting, I could escape my feelings of inadequacy. I didn't have to think about how I wasn't the best basketball player, the fastest kid in gym class, or the best student in school.

• • •

Lifting had provided this escape since fifth grade, and it started with a gift. The weight bench from Mom and Dad was awesome and had everything. The red and white vinyl repelled the sweat I'd worked up. It was a solid, blue metal frame construction. I could do bench presses and leg extensions. The supports could be moved and adjusted so I could do squats. It even came with smaller bars for arm curls. The sand-filled weights were gray, and I thought I would never be as happy as the day Dad brought home the sand and filled them up. He showed me how to use the wrench to secure the weight plates. We set the bench up in the basement. It was largely unfinished and frequently colder than the rest of the house, but I think I practically wanted to move downstairs.

When I was lifting, I felt like I was in charge. What happened was under my control. I was doing something to be a bigger and better version of myself. I felt soreness and started to push through. I figured out alternating workouts because sore muscles needed a chance to rest. As I started to find the weight easier to lift, I was hooked. I couldn't see the changes just yet, but knew I was getting stronger as I added weight or repetitions. Day by day I got better. I started to run a little. Not anything long distance, but I realized running to my friend's house to play had to be better than just walking. Even riding my bike changed. Instead of ramps and reckless jumps, bike riding became a different leg workout. On the bench, I controlled the feelings—I could escape not liking school, myself, and the feeling that I disappointed people. Downstairs in the basement I let myself start to dream. Maybe I really could be a professional football player or even go to the Olympics.

And then one day, two thoughts changed everything. The first was something I knew could be a game changer: What if this weight bench was in my room? I could work out whenever I wanted. The next thought was how to make it happen. I went to Dad, thinking he'd see this as brilliant. He seemed to be open to the idea but said what any smart husband knows as the correct response, "Check with your mother."

How could I convince Mom? My room wasn't huge. Somehow, I had to find a space to make it work. The bench wasn't as big as my bed. It was larger than the storage chest where my little stereo was set up. My stereo! I thought, I could play music while working out! This idea was getting better by the minute. But I'd have to convince Mom. How and where could I put this gift from heaven into my room? Then it hit me. The answer was there all along.

My room had two side-by-side closets. The one on the left had my clothes, shoes, athletic equipment, and the other treasured artifacts a boy would need to access. The one on the right was full of clothes my parents used to wear. It was where polyester fashions of the '60s and '70s went to die. There were suits in there I had never seen my dad wear. The dresses were clearly too big for my sisters, and I had never seen my mom wear these. The floor was covered with high heels and wing tips, a virtual shoe store from years gone by.

This closet was so full of clothes, the bar for holding hangers sagged under the weight. So much so that at some point it had detached from the wall and Dad propped it up with a two-by-four. And as if a golden aura was beaming from this vault of outdated fashion, I knew how I would convince Mom. I brought her into my room, and I'm sure I thanked her again for the weight bench. She already knew how much I was using it and didn't seem surprised when I shared my plan to bring it into my room so I could use it more.

Even though my mom was hard on me about school, she was at least fair and respectful when she said, "Well, Kevin, that's a fine idea, but you don't really have room up here." The following seconds would hold the six words of her motherly question and simultaneously fall right into my well-thought-out plan. She asked, "Exactly where would you put it?"

I responded, "I was thinking over here in this extra closet." Like a prosecuting attorney, I dramatically opened the doors and said, "I looked in it, and it's just full of old clothes, shoes, and stuff you and Dad don't use anymore. Plus, it's just so full the pole you hang stuff on got jerked outta the wall."

She was sort of stunned and had nothing to say, so like a professional wrestler with his opponent on the ropes, I just kept going.

I said, "Looks like Dad had to hold it up with this piece of wood." Pointing at it, I may have even raised an eyebrow as I said,

"It doesn't look very safe. I kinda thought like you make us kids give away our old clothes, maybe you and Dad could do the same. My bench and all the weights could fit right in there."

I stopped talking out loud and thought to myself, And with that, the prosecution rests, your honor. I knew Perry Mason himself could not have come up with a more thoughtful and foolproof argument. Mom was silent. I couldn't tell if she was proud of me and compiling a list of potential law schools, or if she was embarrassed to have been called out on this stash of stuff. Within the week, not all but enough of the clothes had been moved, and my bench was up from the basement.

From then on, I'd set the alarm on the digital Casio watch I didn't like to wear. The beeping could wake me and still be quiet so Mom and Dad wouldn't know I was up. It was surprisingly easy to get up in the middle of the night. I'd go to the closet and very quietly pull out the weight bench and start lifting. In the dark, I would lift and feel like I was in charge, getting myself bigger and stronger. On one hand, I was free to chase those NFL and Olympic dreams. On the other hand, I was doing something to cover all my perceived glaring weaknesses. I didn't think I'd ever match up to the sports hero I saw my dad to be. I felt I was never as smart as Mom thought I should be. My older sister verbally diminished me. My experiences in the church to this point kept reinforcing to me that I was just a bad person, a sinner. The weight of my inner thoughts and secrets was crushing. No parent, no God, could love me for what was going on within me. But night after night I convinced myself I was doing something good there on the bench. It was something to make me stronger and maybe better. Maybe strong enough to remove the secret burdens I carried in my mind, in my heart, in the book bag, and in my athletic bag.

●　　●　　●

Do you remember school? I'm thinking maybe I went about school all wrong. The way I figured it was if you got the teacher to like you, you'd do all right when it came to grading. There's a big hole in this kind of logic. Most teachers genuinely like their students and want them to do well. At least the ones I've known. Still, even the best of teachers can't see it all. What were the hurts you stuffed deep into the bags you carried between home and school? What were the secret bruises you didn't know how to share with anyone? What were the personal weights you tried to lift in secret all on your own? We all experience one of those teachers who made us feel like we couldn't do anything right. Just like we have different names for the schools we attend, those thoughts also have names. These days we have terms to provide perspective and help us understand things, like negative self-talk and poor self-image. Back then a lot of us just knew we had an inexpressible ache. Why were they so hard to figure out and where did they come from? The Church Lady from Saturday Night Live would've answered, "Oh, I don't know, perhaps Satan!" Pierced lips and darting eyes aside, growing up in our families can be tough at any age. Both for children and the ones trying to figure out being an adult. We convince ourselves it will magically all work out. We also know that sometimes it doesn't. But with just a slight shift we can see the good news too.

Hopefully, we also remember those teachers who helped us believe we could do anything. My coaches were teachers and some of the most inspiring people I've met. As much as they pushed the right buttons and motivated me to be my best, they were still human, and didn't come close to Jesus' ability to instruct and encourage. Jesus also was a teacher, although He certainly wasn't like any of the teachers of His day. In fact, He kept turning their lessons upside down. Sort of like Rocky taught me to do my sit-ups. As much as our favorite teachers and coaches inspired us, we know they don't compare to Jesus. Maybe that's because their message wasn't as simple as Jesus'. He didn't care about conjugating verbs, exotic blocking schemes, or the periodic table. Most of us spent thirteen years between kindergarten and high school graduation. Some of us studied more in college. Think of all the teachers, professors, the subjects we studied and likely have forgotten about. Jesus taught His friends, and they spent a lifetime talking about three things. Faith, hope, and love. Jesus and His friends taught the greatest of those is love.

As simple as it may seem, as educated as we think ourselves to be, we aren't much different from the audiences back in Jesus' day. We can often miss the point. Maybe if we think back, there is something simple we could recall. Something to hold as a reminder when things aren't so simple. If we just had a heavy anchor for when the waters of life get choppy. Something to act as a key to let us out of the cage of our old thinking. There was a song I remember. We sometimes forget all the words. It started with something simple like "Jesus loves me, this I know." Jesus' love for us is never an excuse for wrong behavior, hurting others or ourselves. At times our struggles will make us feel crazy or out of control. Jesus's love is calling us out from our closets where we feverishly attempt to work out the impossible problems on our own. He calls us out from under the scars and scabs of our hurts where we like to hide. He says bring it all to me and surrender, for I am setting you free from your cage. The prize is better than any championship status. It will not fade or go out of style. It is His complete, consuming, unconditional love.

CHAPTER 15

What is a Quitter?

There is a reason you won't be reading a section about my not-so-illustrious track-and-field career. Despite having the same last name, I did not inherit the same track-and-field gene as my "brother" Carl—you know him as the winner of nine Olympic gold medals. Maybe because it was spring, maybe because I wanted to discover another sport, or maybe because all the pretty girls were doing it, I had decided to go out for junior high track. Now here's the deal—I don't think they ever cut anyone from junior high track.

If you showed up and improved on a certain time, you could "earn" your team sweats. Being a typical boy, it was rare I said no to a challenge. (Remind me later to tell you the story of how I swallowed a live worm for ten dollars.) Free sweats sounded like a school-endorsed double-dog dare. Mom signed whatever paper was required and I hopped the bus driving prospective track stars to the high school track where we practiced.

We had run our first time; I beat it the next day and earned those school-issued track-and-field sweats. I remember being a little surprised to see Coach Colls on the field. I think he might have been the one who handed me the maroon sweats with white lettering. I say surprised because despite being an elementary school teacher, it turns out, he was also our junior high coach.

Before dry-erase boards or white board projectors existed, we had the real deal, old-school chalkboards. Every now and then a teacher would accidentally hold the chalk the wrong way or maybe press too hard, and the screeching shrill of a thousand fingernails would shiver down the spine of everyone in the class. Despite the possibility of the spine-altering, ear-shattering sound, there was plenty to like about old-school chalk.

When I was younger, my teachers had a magic wand for chalk. This contraption typically had a wooden handle with five metal prongs. Each prong was about six inches long and could grasp a piece of chalk. Sort of like a metallic version of our teachers' fingers. Our music teacher would draw perfectly straight lines and use them as a musical score. My English teacher would use the same device but with only two pieces. She added a dotted line in between for showing us how to write capital and lower-case letters. As we got older there would come times when the teacher would call us up front to spell a word or work out a math answer on the board. There was something about those moments when they called your name and handed you their piece of chalk. Sometimes it was like the passing of the baton. With each passing of the chalk baton came a double-edged sword. On one edge was the feeling of power as if we were somehow now in charge of the class. The other edge carried a sense of responsibility and the weight of every eyeball in the room.

I suppose the same could be said for dry-erase markers, but there was just something almost magical about the feel of a piece of chalk in your hands, and inevitably, on your hands. Each of us would rub it off on our pants or purposefully on our faces. We wore each chalk smudge as a badge of sorts, somehow acknowledging we were special because we'd been chosen to help lead the class. But far and away the coolest thing about chalkboards was the eraser cleaning machine.

Our school got one of these when our principal grew tired of seeing eraser marks all along the walls on the back side of the school. This is where our teachers would routinely send students to bang chalk dust out of erasers. Yes, there was more than one occasion when erasers were smashed together like cymbals. Instead of a crashing sound there would be a cloud-size puff of chalk. I also have it on good authority there were occasions when erasers where thrown, not like shot puts but more like baseballs. I also "heard" occasionally that there might have been an eraser war or two. Erasers had to be soft on one side to effectively remove the chalk, but on the other side they were firm and usually had thick paper labels. I suppose it made it easier to properly grip them to erase something. I know—I mean, I heard—they were easy to grip during the unsanctioned eraser wars. During battle, there would be running and chasing like sprinters around a track. Occasionally the backs of two erasers would meet in midair, resulting in a loud crack like a starter's gun. The sound would startle us (I mean startle the people participating in such silliness) and typically prompted our return to class. Perhaps persistent rumors of such battles also prompted the school's decision to acquire the eraser cleaner.

The new machine meant instead of banging the erasers outside, we took them to our school custodian. Like Merlin in the White

Mountains, he oversaw this magical machine, which could handle both white and yellow chalk. We would hand him our dusty erasers and he would run them back and forth over the machine. Each pass extracted the chalk within seconds, vanquishing the ghosts of spelling words and math problems gone by. He'd quickly finish each one, making them good as new. He then handed them back and sent us on our way to return to class. As fascinated as we were with the new machine, we sort of missed the epic eraser battles and the challenge of removing chalk marks from our clothes. Or at least those were the reports I'd been told.

●　　●　　●

I don't think Mr. Colls ever took advantage of this new technology. He'd established a reputation for launching those chalk-filled erasers at students who weren't listening. He never missed. There always seemed to be a puff of smoke around the kid who got caught not listening. Somehow, I escaped having him as a teacher in elementary school, but here he was, our junior high track coach.

Track was a spring sport and on cue my allergies flared up. I was particularly good at getting sinus infections. They are horrible. It's hard to breathe, the hacking cough, and the colors of mucus … let's just say, Crayola doesn't make that shade of crayon. Having earned my sweats and made it through week one, I stumbled into week two with a raging sinus infection. As if this was not challenging enough, there was a cold snap in the weather, and we actually needed to be wearing those sweats. Did I mention the pretty girls were running track?

I think they must have been my motivation to continue. As the week went on, the coughing and hacking only grew worse. To top it off, all the girls I liked were racing past me. I was beyond embarrassed and determined for the first time in my life I was going to quit. This was huge, because in my family, we were told you don't quit. You can see the season through and then decide to not play again, but you don't quit.

I had convinced myself my dad would understand this one. I started to rehearse my lines: "Dad, I was so bad at running track, girls were beating me!" Surely, the Mr. Studly Dudly award winner would understand my logic. Yes, it was wrong to blame my quitting on the fact girls were beating me. I was in eighth grade and my brain was still developing. The fact that girls were just as good, if not better than me, was quickly becoming self-evident. In the absence of having sinus replacement surgery, it quickly became clear track and field was not going to be a part of my future. After yet another spell of hacking and coughing up shades of dark green, blue, brown, and yellow stuff, I took off my sweats. I folded them up and walked them over to Coach Colls.

My parents taught us to not use swear words. However, on occasion we certainly heard them pepper their communication with these very same words. Maybe it was because my parents cussed, or my embarrassment from girls beating me or perhaps it was sheer exhaustion from coughing and hacking. Regardless of the reason, I walked up to Coach Colls and told him, "I quit."

He didn't say anything. He just looked at me, and it was then I started to question whether Dad would understand my logic. I no sooner finished the thought and the next coughing spell hit. What came out of me seemed to be the size of an oyster. It fell to the ground and maybe it's what inspired me to likewise toss my sweats toward the feet of the coach who clearly was not acknowledging my crisis. I was at my wits end and said, "You need to give these to somebody who can do this shi—." Yes, I actually did say the word to an adult. As I walked away there was no turning around and no attempt to convince me otherwise.

Maybe Coach knew I'd learn from this. Could he somehow see into the future? Did he already know years later I'd move back to the area, with a chance to help him coach the junior high team? Was he already planning his entrance?

Years later it sure seemed like it. Right on cue Coach Colls walked into the office. The coach I'd been talking to started to introduce me. Coach Colls was already smiling and recognized me. He tilted his head to the side and said, "Oh yes, Mr. Lewis, I remember a certain day on the track with you." We shared a laugh as I explained the track story to the other coach.

On the track that day, I was just grateful there was no eraser heading my way. I walked home from practice, as the high school was just a mile and a half from our house. I rationalized it was nothing for a newly former track star. I got home, shared the story with Mom, making sure to leave out the precise verbiage of my last phrase to Coach. I guess she called Dad and told him he didn't need to pick me up. To my surprise, I think my parents understood or thought I was learning something. The fact I'd quit didn't come up, at least not then.

● ● ●

My coach and my parents were right. I certainly did learn something from quitting. Although it wasn't until years later when I'd met a new friend. He told me he makes it a habit to quit something every week. He explained if tasks, situations, or habits are taking you away from your purpose, it's better to quit. That's when it dawned on me, there might be something to this quitting. Still, I don't know too many people who want to be labeled a quitter. It's not exactly deemed a positive character trait. When I owned a gym and coached girls' gymnastics, I learned a thing or two I had not previously known or considered. One of those was the nickname the girls had for people who wore sweatpants and sweatshirts. They called them quitters by explaining the person just gave up or quit caring what other people think. As crazy as it may sound, I think to a certain extent Jesus wants us to be a quitter.

I know. I can hear you thinking. You are racing back through Bible stories we've all heard and thinking the Bible is pretty clear. We are supposed to persevere, endure, and keep running the race set before us. You are thinking I may have inhaled too much chalk dust. While that last part is still to be determined, let me put your mind at ease. Yes, the Bible does talk about persistence and running the race. We all want to cut through the ribbon as we cross the final finish line. Who wouldn't want to be a part of such a glorious cloud of witnesses? And the Bible does, indeed, teach us to not only expect, but endure hard times. Countless stories tell tales of tribes of people wandering through a desert of difficulties and facing the temptation to quit, turn around, go home, and give up.

I am not saying Jesus wants us to run away from our responsibility or slip into sweats, be they from the school track team or not. The older I get the more examples I see of the bad sort of quitting. People walk away from marriages, their careers, and some even walk from their faith. I think if we are honest with ourselves, the idea of quitting is not as uncommon as we think. When we are young, we want to quit living with our parents. If we are single, we want to quit being single and get married. As we age, we want to quit overeating or quit working and retire. We know God wants us to quit the obvious things like cussing, drinking, or eating in excess. Or perhaps we need to quit thinking about cheating on our taxes, our spouse, or running over the driver who cut us off in traffic. We even see examples in the Bible where God or Jesus quite literally called someone to quit.

Don't believe me? Check with Jonah. He kept avoiding Nineveh, at least until a whale intervened. What about Zacchaeus? Jesus yelled up to him and told him to quit being a monkey, hanging out in a tree. Check with Andrew, Peter, James, and John. Jesus called them in such a way, they lay down their nets, left family behind, and quit their jobs on the spot to follow Him. And perhaps most importantly, be sure to check in with Lazarus, Jairus' daughter, and the son of the widow Nain. Jesus literally called them to stop being dead. I think in a similar way He might be calling us too.

At the heart of each of our decisions is why? Why did Zacchaeus come down from the tree? Because Jesus wanted to spend time with him, love on him, and get him over the hurdle of cheating people. Why did those disciples drop their nets as if they were heavy shot puts? Because Jesus's voice pierced their hearts like a javelin when He said those two words follow me. Why did Jesus call those people back to life? Yes, because of His mercy but clearly He also had greater things planned for them. And when I look at the mess we live in, I think back to those wounds. Our screaming voices and steaming piles of mess make me wonder, why would God come up with a plan and send Jesus to be with us? We know the answer is because God loves us.

God doesn't quit on us. And guess what? He's not interested if you've been living in a pigpen or hanging in a tree. He's not concerned if you've been stealing from others or giving your fortune away. He doesn't care about our mistakes and wrong choices. Speaking of which, the worm wasn't worth the ten bucks. And why? Because worms are slimy and meant for catching the fish, not to feed us. Taking shortcuts won't work with worms, and even our best, most prayed-about plan needs a change. Because God is always calling us to know His heart more. The more we focus on His heart, the more we are open to His idea of how we are being shaped and chiseled. Like a master sculptor, He's hard at work. Maybe we feel like we're aimlessly circling the track, or perhaps we think we should be on the podium by now. The truth is we may not yet see the many small changes He erases each day. And yes, there are going to be times when big chunks and changes are chiseled away. It's going to hurt worse than running a mile with a raging sinus infection in the spring. But we can be assured of this: He will see His work to completion. He won't leave us hacking or halfway done. His Spirit is always with us. We are never alone. God doesn't quit.

CHAPTER 16

"You're Better Than That!"

My short-lived track career played a part in how I met Coach George. There are three things you should know about Coach George before I tell you how we met. His family ran a restaurant, and I thought the fact that both our families were in the restaurant business would provide me a potential "in" with him. It did not. There was a wicked rumor the man's name was George George George. We weren't about to ask him, and it ended up not being true. But the most notable characteristic was his fiery reputation for how he ran his classroom, even tighter and stricter than Coach Colls.

I think to fully understand our eighth-grade, healthy fear of this man and his reputation, I have to tell you a story from a day during my junior year in high school. Or as we called it, the day he destroyed our trading cards. McDonald's was offering collector cards of pro football players. Now if any of us needed more motivation to chow down fast food, this was it. The commercial on TV featured well-known professional football players from actual game footage where they were pointing, celebrating, and tackling each other. There were obvious voice-overs that kept declaring, "I got your card, I got your card!"

We just had to see it once, and we mimicked this every day at practice. And when I say every day, I truly mean every day. Eventually we drove Coach George past his tipping point. He blew his whistle and screamed at the top of his lungs, "I don't wanna hear another thing about these stupid cards!"

We all stopped and stood in silence, but he went on.

"You see I got 'em, I got 'em all, I got all the cards and I am tearing them all up!"

His eyes were on fire and his hands furiously flew in front of his chest as if tearing every trading card ever made in the history of mankind. He pretended to throw them up in the air and then ended his rant with, "There are no more cards! They're all gone!"

This was the fire-breathing coach we knew and would grow to love. As fate would have it, I first met Coach George not on an athletic field, not even in a classroom, but in the hallway of junior high, where he taught civics, before he became a high school football coach. All these years later, I still remember our first talk.

It was in between classes; some friends and I were chatting about whatever junior high school boys talk about by our lockers. You know the stereotypical scene on television or in the movies when a group of people are talking and something, or someone is approaching the group. Maybe they start getting wide-eyed or go silent and begin to back away. Everyone sees what's coming. That is everyone but the one person who has his back turned in the wrong direction. Well, I was the guy. I read the faces of my friends and just like in the movies I turned around.

There he was. He was equally as intimidating to this eighth-grader as Godzilla, the Terminator, and Rambo all wrapped up in one. Coach George was walking toward the group as if on a mission. And while it would not be a surprise for a teacher to be clearing a group from the hall, it quickly became clear this was not his mission. Within nanoseconds, Coach George was standing very close to me. I could hear the scattering of closing lockers and the shuffling footsteps of my friends as they scattered. I was his target.

However, he simply and quietly said, "Hey, I heard about what you did at track."

I think I looked away and tried to shrug it off.

He added, "You're better than that!"

There was no fire, no fury, no nothing. He turned and walked into his classroom.

It was then, I realized, before today I'd never muttered a word to this man. I was truly amazed he even knew who I was or that I existed. But his words would stick with me. You're better than that.

•　　•　　•

I only played one year of youth football. I was maybe eight years old and got knocked out cold during a game called Bull in the Ring. I survived and finished out the season. I also recall watching a football game with my dad. I believe it was the running back for the Philadelphia Eagles who was being run out of bounds and his arm or collarbone was broken. That was it for me. If my favorite sports team heroes could get hurt, and I got hurt, my brain rationalized living without football and without pain was better than playing. I'd stick with wrestling.

Don't we all have those moments? Maybe it's not a football game, but we have those hurts. You know, the ones we don't like to talk about. The ones that quietly fester and occasionally sneak up on us from time to time, attempting to drag us back to the moment of injury. I'd been hurt and built a wall of reasons to not play football. While it meant I wouldn't play in college like my dad, I figured not playing football would be playing it safe. And maybe that's what Coach George's message was all about. I attempted to stay under the radar the rest of eighth grade. I didn't know all of my play-it-safe thinking would be changed one spring day close to the end of the school year.

I was half dozing in-and-out, partly asleep, partly there. I know it was springtime because the windows were cracked open, the sun was shining, and a gentle warm breeze was drifting into class. I want to say it was Ms. Brown's eighth grade civics class, but even that is fuzzy in my brain. I do recall the crackle of the PA system stirring me to a more alert state.

The secretary's voice always came on with the same lead in, "Teachers, please pardon the interruption."

Now typically this was for some boring announcement that rarely had anything to do with me, but this one was different. The voice continued, "Coach Highfill from the high school is here to speak to any eighth-grade boys who might be interested in playing football next year. Please dismiss any eighth-grade boy to the auditorium to meet with Coach Highfill and learn about this opportunity."

I think I was wiping drool from the corner of my mouth when I started to review her message in my brain. Did she say, Please excuse any eighth-grade BOY ... to the auditorium ... to learn more about football? CHECK. I'm an eighth-grade boy. Would I like to get out of class? Ummmm, big check again. Did I at least know what football was, and did I mention I could get out of class to go listen to Coach what's-his-face? Check, check, checkity, check-check!

The next thing I knew my previously semi-sleeping body was standing up to join what seemed to be an army of boys. I knew some of them. There were kids I played with in the neighborhood and some kids who were the star athletes of our school. But I also gathered rather quickly, I wasn't the only boy thinking, Ha, free pass out of class! We meandered down the halls of our old junior high.

This had been the original high school, but the county re-purposed it to be our junior high in the late '60s. Sometimes it was confusing to walk down the halls and see pictures of the graduating class of such and such. The entire graduating class fit on one of those single oversized photos. I'd have to go back and check, but those pictures were old. Some were faded, some had small tears, and all were black-and-white images of odd-looking teenagers. They certainly didn't look like the motley crew of kids getting out of class to go listen to a football coach. As I walked past the stares from the pictures of these graduates from years gone by, something told me they, too, had pulled such epic stunts. Out of class for free, wow, I felt so smart.

My smart smugness quickly faded away when Coach Highfill walked onto the stage. What I saw was a cross between Dabo Swinney, the Clemson football coach, and Pete Carroll, one-time USC coach and currently coaching in the NFL with the Seahawks. I realize not everyone gets geeked out about football like I do, I get it. Just know in the moment, Highfill had a glow about him. Maybe it was just his youthful confidence or the spring sunshine peeking in through the auditorium windows past the thick curtains. I don't really remember much of what he said, but rather how he spoke.

Something in this man's voice reached past my façade. It reached through the suddenly not-so-epic track team sweats stunt. It's one of those things you hear people talk about when they describe a life-changing experience. I don't know how long Coach talked to us that day. It could've been as short as five or ten minutes, but it could've just as easily been five to ten hours. There's a cheesy line from a movie: "You had me at hello." I would only add the phrase, "My name is Coach Highfill." It wasn't a man crush. It wasn't anything other than the sound in his voice. It read the room, found me and my play-it-safe thinking. It convinced the little kid who'd been knocked out to get back up. It spoke to the kid who felt he wasn't good enough and quit. His voice convinced me to get off the sidelines of life, to get back in the game and try again. As much as I am thankful for lessons learned from my coaches, these men weren't God. To be clear, none of them ever asserted they were. Still, just like my coaches could speak to me, I think God is still speaking to us.

● ● ●

God doesn't always speak audibly. Sure, Moses had the burning bush. We can't put God in a box and be convinced He wouldn't communicate this way again. However, I think we can agree it's rare. I do think God still whispers to us (mainly internally) through scripture and the teachers or spiritual coaches He puts along our path. The spirit nudges, asking if we can trust. We might not have the burning bush like Moses. We might not get the visit from a golden, glowing, angel telling us what to do. I do think these days God more readily uses living people than angels to call out to us, to speak into us, to help us see the gifts we don't even know are inside of us. When Jesus's mother was young, she met an angel named Gabriel. He's the one who told Mary she'd have a baby.

And yes, in a slightly less angelic way, I got to meet two coaches. Do I think God sent a teacher who wasn't one of mine? Is it possible that despite my not knowing this teacher, he could a) find me in a busy school hallway, and b) remind me that I was "better than that"? Is it possible God used my choice to quit, an unspeakable thing in my house, to orchestrate delivery of a message? Could God work through the announcement from a school secretary, which prompted me to jokingly take advantage of it and just get out of class? Could God combine all of these random things to allow me to meet someone else who would challenge me with a voice that called out gifts I didn't even know I had? Well, based upon how He's done things since the beginning of time, I'd say heck yeah!

Here's a truth: everybody has a gift. Granted, there are those who seem to have been sprinkled with a little extra something. In my time coaching gymnastics, I got to watch some very talented young people do some incredible things. But none of them started with a high-end skill. They all started with forward rolls and handstands, and frequently crashed to their heads. They started with cartwheels that nearly took off my head. Most of their skills only came after many lead-up drills, tons of strength work, and focusing on proper skill shapes. Add in a fair dose of time and effort, and eventually skills came. Then there was Simone. A gymnast so well-known worldwide, I don't have to mention her last name. Even the most casual observer of the sport can see it. I'm not by any means undercutting the hours of training or years of hard work she's done, but clearly, she is a generational talent with gifts of courage and ability beyond the norm.

Who is it in your world? Who have you seen, heard, read, or listened to? Who blows your socks off like Simone? Was it a preacher or schoolteacher? Is there a musical group, a dancer, a symphony, or an artist you find so talented? They write the songs, perform the dances, and paint pictures that routinely speak to your heart when words fail. They do this so consistently, you make certain to download every song, enjoy each performance, and buy every book. There's no question, some of the things we call gifts are things we chose, we pursued, developed, and got better. And still not all of us change the world through art or sport. Very few will have crowds screaming their name or have specific event skills named after them like Simone. But I bet there are many more of us who tried something, maybe we even went on and practiced it for many years, and even if we don't change the world, the experience, changed us. Maybe like me, your experience of youth sports scared you. But for whatever reason you tried again. Most of us won't get to play our sports as a pro or even in college, but because of a teacher, a coach, or someone else investing and sharing themselves, you changed. You got better.

We all have gifts. Some are going to be artists, athletes, or known worldwide for something else. Some will be those teachers and coaches who maybe while we experience them seem to have the golden aura around them. They are the ones who reach kids by speaking into them, by calling them out to be better, to not settle for playing it safe. Some of us will be lesser-known for things like visiting our neighbors and friends when they are in the hospital. Some will be known as the person who went and visited those imprisoned. Some are known as the ones always organizing the blood drive, the fundraiser, or the person quietly spending time serving others at the soup kitchen. Whatever it is, the world needs more of you. Don't believe your gift is too small. Don't kid yourself and believe the experiences you've had are just random or insignificant. Don't fall for the lies that seek to distract us from using the gifts we've been given. What you do, matters.

I'm a lot older now. It's been decades since I played any organized sport on a team. It's been even longer since I was challenged to "be better" in between classes in a junior high school hallway. I haven't heard a halftime or pregame speech in three and a half decades. But God is still in the practice of putting "coaches" along our path. God is still calling out to us. He wants us to know Him better and He can't wait to use your gifts to make Himself known to others.

CHAPTER 17

Wrestle to Win

I both liked and failed to appreciate cheerleaders when I was an athlete. I liked them because, well, they were pretty! But I failed to appreciate their attempts to cheer and inspire me from the edges of the wrestling mat. Their smiling, encouraging faces were temporarily lost to me each time they performed a particular cheer. It went, "Wrestle, wrestle! Wrestle to win!" There would be the sound of four rapid hand claps—clap-clap-clap-clap—and the cheer would repeat over and over and over. I remember their arm movements, too, but they were as confusing to me as the meaning of the words.

I am sure my friends who were cheerleaders were very well-intentioned. We were the Terriers and they were equally dogged in their determined attempts to support us in so many incredible ways. They decorated our lockers on match day, supplied us with our favorite candy bars for after weigh-ins, and one year they even helped design a pillowcase with our wrestling logo on it. I still have mine and even framed it. I most appreciate the fact that they approached our coach to learn about words or phrases used in wrestling. This was all very nice. But when I was wrestling and they started this cheer, my mind would wander from the match and just shy of sarcasm would ask questions like, Do they think I endure early morning runs, two-and-half-hour daily practices, including holidays and occasional weekends to not win? Do they think I choose cutting weight, conditioning, seemingly endless repetitive drills, black eyes, bruises, sprained and sometimes bloodied body parts so that I can lose?

I was young, full of adrenaline and macho bravado—maybe this is why I wasn't a fan of the cheer—but like a lot of folks, I at least hoped my goals and intentions were obvious. Do any of us set about a task thinking we don't want to be successful in one form or another? It took a few years, some missteps, a few poor choices, and a couple of outright stings, to fully appreciate the valuable role "cheerleaders" serve in our lives. And just like it took me a while to appreciate cheers, we've all had days start out with something like spilled milk or dog food. Yes, I said spilled dog food.

● ● ●

I recently decided to adopt a dog, just before Christmas. I checked all the online listings of local kennels but had no luck. My search continued and I found a kennel in a neighboring state. They were running a Home for the Holidays event and had given the dogs holiday-themed names. I suppose they were trying to be cute, but it was obvious these were temporary names to further the event theme. The dogs I would be visiting were named Rudolph, Cornelius, and Brutus. I, too, was at a loss on Brutus and saw no connection to the holidays. Regardless of the dog I would choose, the adoption fee was just twenty-five dollars. After a two-hour drive, I met them one at a time.

Rudolph was a boy with beautiful shepherd markings and a black snout, but he was a bit of a diva and there was just no connection. Next came Brutus and I quickly discovered Brutus must be short for Brutal Grinch. He was massive. Seventy-five pounds of pure muscle. A mix of bulldog and something. He dragged me across the parking lot and back. That was enough for me. Brutus was the perfect dog—for someone else. And then came Cornelius.

He was one of thirty rescued from a particular location. At only six months old he was already forty-seven pounds, but I was told he was one of the smaller dogs. To me, he was big. Until he arrived at the kennel, he'd spent his entire life chained up outside with no human interaction. He had muscles, but was full of fright and scars. The kennel workers told me the only interaction he had with other dogs was when they were attacking him. He was a far cry from the courageous character he'd been named for. His front legs revealed multiple scrapes and bite marks. Under his chin appeared a golf ball–sized something. The attendant told me it was a wound from where another dog bit and held him, but he assured me it had been treated and antibiotics had done their job. There was no infection, just a wound trying to heal.

The dog didn't even want to come outside. He would not make eye contact with me and scurried to a corner at the front of the building where I suppose he felt safe. He was a beautiful mix of golden retriever and Lab, just terribly afraid and scared. In my life I've owned at least seven dogs, and none ever looked as frightened as this. Before meeting him I'd only seen dogs shiver like this in the heart-wrenching commercials asking for a monthly pledge. He and I both needed someone and without hesitation I knew I would adopt him.

About then the shelter volunteer mentioned that if I wanted to take him today, they would waive the fee. I think he was recognizing this poor pup was going to need some work. He was a far cry from the loving, licking, playful puppy children dream of on Christmas Eve. But in the kind offer of a "free" dog, my heart sank, recognizing that the monetary value of this animal was zero. They were literally giving him away.

We know the feeling of being disregarded, tossed to the side, being the target of biting remarks. If it didn't happen in your family, maybe it occurred somewhere during your schooling. Maybe you felt it in junior high over a crush. Maybe it stung when the job, the one you thought was perfect for you, didn't pan out. Perhaps it's when the death certificate of a parent or child was handed to you or arrived in your mailbox. Maybe it was the slam of the gavel when the divorce became final, the false words hurtled by an ex-spouse landed and never let up. Something happened, somebody said something, and the words still weigh heavy on you. They left a wound, not on your chin but in your heart. Keep your chin up is one of those phrases that's easier said than done when it's our heart that is hurting.

While the shelter wouldn't accept anything for the dog, they happily accepted payment for him to be micro-chipped and a modest monetary donation to cover veterinary procedures. This dog had my heart in the first twenty seconds, but it took another twenty minutes until we would be documented and ready for the trip home. While waiting outside, a lady approached and asked if I was the one adopting Cornelius. I confirmed I was, and she reiterated he was not used to people or dogs that weren't trying to hurt him. By the looks of her dirty clothes and the marks on her arms, I assumed she'd been involved in his rescue. She provided further details of what he'd survived.

Eventually the dog and I said our goodbyes to the staff and walked outside—where he promptly ducked under my truck. He was only six months old and had never experienced someone saying, "Hey, buddy, let's go for a car ride." After some coaxing, some treats, only a few growls, and an assist from the kennel staff, he did finally come out. He jumped into the truck and lay down for the trip to a new home.

The first night in my three hundred and ninety-two square foot tiny house, we had a little challenge. He'd get nervous whenever I was within fifteen feet, didn't want his leash off, and rather than sleep on the soft, plush bedding, he chose a towel tossed on the floor. Dogs aren't the only ones who sometimes choose holding on to the harsh and uncomfortable over healing.

The next morning came, and it was time for breakfast. Rather than scoop it out of the fifty-pound bag, I acquired a Tupperware container to hold about a dozen meals. I went to measure out the food and just as I was about to fill the cup, it happened. It was one of those things you see happening in real life but visually it's all slow motion. Somehow the plastic cover had worked loose, and a dozen meals of food flooded out, covered the glass-top stove, spilling down the front and into the cracks between the oven and kitchen cabinets. Cornelius didn't eat all of it but was more than happy to assist with cleanup. If dogs think like us, and I suspect they do, I hope he thought, Maybe, just maybe, this human won't hurt me or let me be hurt.

This was just the beginning of his loving demeanor starting to emerge. Like the parent of a newborn, I discovered a new facet each day. I tried to call him Cornelius, but it didn't even tweak his ears. Because of his large size, I tried calling him Moose—same response, nothing. With his coloring and muscularity, I thought he looked like a lion minus the mane, so I tried Mufasa. But he didn't respond to anything. So I just called him my buddy, thinking his name would present itself over time.

I think back on those first moments we met: the sinking feeling of not being valued, the emptiness of giving and giving while receiving nothing in return, and the thankfulness from just happening to find each other. It might sound odd to suggest God had a hand in allowing our paths to cross. Really? The same hand to cast stars and planets. The same hand to separate oceans, dry land, and the sky. The same hand to define night and day. Why would this hand have anything to do with me and a dog meeting? Supposedly He's able to work all things for the good of those who love Him. And even though some people still get hung up on whether animals will be in heaven (pssssst, I think they will be) maybe it's not so far-fetched He'd be involved in our meeting.

The same hand who did all those things also created all life and, in fact, brought it to man to name each animal. I'm not suggesting having a pet is better than our human relationships. Still the connection between humans, animals, and Creator is real. I know this dog and I had both been through the ringer. We'd both been hurt and tied down. And there was a very real correlation between our life experiences. We both had scars on the outside and some tucked deep on the inside too. We both needed a buddy. Then it happened. About ninety days in, I was watching a story about mountain bikes on television. He was half sleeping in the seat next to me when I asked out loud, "Does that look like fun, buddy?" His eyes opened, his ears tweaked, and his head lifted. He heard a voice that showed him love and recognized his name, so Buddy it would be.

●　　●　　●

Did you know there are four buddies credited as creators of the mountain bike? One was credited with introducing the first purpose-built mountain bike in 1978. Then there was a business partnership between three other guys who went on to create and mass produce the frames we now know as mountain bikes. One of them was named Tom Ritchey.[4]

In the '70s and '80s I was riding my bike, trying to stay out of trouble and playing games of kick-the-can in our darkened neighborhood. Meanwhile, Tom Ritchey was doing incredible

[4]See footnote in Appendix

things in cycling. He raced on a national level, made his own bike parts, and when road racing was banned in California, he and his friends quite literally went off-road. That's when he first saw a mountain bike. He was so taken he asked his friend to make one just like it. Their business formed and took off, but just as quickly dissolved. In the '90s Tom ran his own company. He focused on designing specific bike components, additionally creating over five hundred hand-built frames each year. Now you'd think a guy so successful would have it all. But in the early 2000's, Tom's first wife left him. Ouch, show of hands? I know many of us can relate to that sting. Maybe you do too.

Just like each of us, Tom had internal battles; he has described himself as being self-centered and insecure. Even in that scrambled emotional state, he knew he would become bitter or better. He credits the people who expressed their belief in him with helping his choice to choose the latter. He didn't give up, and didn't lose hope. He was persistent and kept pedaling forward. In 2005, Tom had been invited by a friend to go on an African bike trip. Tom rolled through Rwanda, and this changed his life. Rwanda had experienced years of civil war and bloodshed—something about this trip, and these people, clicked in Tom like the playing cards in my spokes.

Tom returned to Rwanda the next year and started a bike race. Thousands of folks came out to watch the race, and soon a national cycling program was launched. The nation's government even got behind this movement as an attempt to promote the positive changes in their country. Now, in America if a puppy isn't on your kid's wish list, a bike probably is. In Rwanda only about one in every one hundred people even have a bike. And the ones they do have are typically broken down and hardly useful, given the lay of the land. About this time, Tom met a doctor involved with something many of us enjoy, coffee. This relationship led to the development and building of the Coffee Bike. It not only helped coffee growers get their product to the wash plants, but also allowed healthcare workers get to their clinics and patients much more efficiently.

How is it these ingredients can come together and brew up something wonderful? I'm talking about Tom, not coffee—his lifelong passion for cycling; the bitter dash and briny burn of a failed marriage; the aroma and flavor of belief in him from a few good friends brewing up a new man; the drizzle of an invite to attend a bike ride on the other side of the planet; how the grind of a bike race helped dress the wounds and cup the heart of a country healing from the flames of bloodshed, unrest, and civil war. How is it all of these are whisked and whipped into something to improve patient care by improving transportation for healthcare workers and, yes, allows so many something as simple as a better cup of coffee? Two years later Tom met and married his second wife. And to no one's surprise, he made a special tandem bike for them to enjoy.

Here's my point. Life is better with companions and cheerleaders. God didn't make us to live a life alone. We need companions—primarily people, but pups count too. Sometimes we need to be a friend and cheer on others in our life. At other times we need them to remind us of hope, higher purpose, and who we are becoming. And maybe, in the dark moments when life throws a curveball, we fail to appreciate the cheerleaders among us. We can recognize our childhood ambitions for a puppy and a bike are not a bad place to restart.

None of this is all that shocking in light of what Jesus said. He told us we had to have the hearts of children if we wanted the kingdom of heaven. Despite our grown-up ability to acquire pets and pedals, sometimes we lose sight of their simple goodness in the storms of growing up or grown-up hurts. But what we cannot ever lose sight of is hope. At times we can remind ourselves because we hold His strong guiding light within us. It's there, even if we don't see it right away. There are going to be times, when it seems too dark, like we aren't going to find the way out. This is precisely when we need the outside reminders coming alongside our wrestling mats. We need the bright torches of friends believing in us. We need to brew up new dreams, be bold enough to try again, and maybe try new things. Perhaps most importantly, we need to listen and heed the wisdom in the words of those cheering us on. Wrestle, wrestle, wrestle to win!

CHAPTER 18

Wedge-Buster

My football career was nowhere as stellar as my father's. I'm proud of his football exploits, and maybe because of them, I did have one day, I repeat, one day with the quarterbacks. But suffice to say, I did not have my father's arm or touch in the passing game.

My freshman season on the JV squad didn't result in any noteworthy stats. I played running back and defensive back. I don't recall getting in a game for a single play. My sophomore year wasn't much better. Despite an offseason of lifting weights and working out, I think I only gained about five pounds. I still thought I was a running back and I got to play during a game. The ball came to me on two consecutive plays. The first was a two-yard gain, the next a three-yard loss. I know, not exactly screaming star running back. My career rushing stat still stands at a whopping negative one yard. I did see stars though: it was when I was knocked out during a Monday practice. I don't remember who hit me, but I know it was a Monday. Because of the hit, I was told to sit out the twelve-minute run we did every week.

Getting knocked out or knocked down in life has a way of taking a shot at our pride. I don't think there's anything wrong with trying to do things in a manner that one can be proud of. We all want to do things well. I suppose pride is another lesson in tension. We just knew, every Monday, we had to bring our running shoes to the track. It didn't matter if it was hot or pouring down rain, we were going to run. Unless of course, you'd been knocked unconscious.

At the end of nearly three hours of beating on each other, we'd quickly have to swap our cleats for running shoes and report to our designated lane. Running backs and receivers ran on the farthest outside lane. The tight ends and some other position players were in the middle lane and of course the hogs, the linemen in the trenches, ran the shortest distance on the inside. Each group had a coach who ran in front and set the pace. I think it was Coach George who ran with the lineman. Coach Highfill ran with the tight ends and quarterbacks. And Coach Trent ran on the outer lane with backs and receivers. This was simultaneously the coolest and most twisted thing. I thought it was cool how our coaches, who had nothing to prove to us, jumped in and set the pace. It was twisted because, to my recollection, they were all good at running and pushed us to keep up. There was a highlight to report from my sophomore year, and while it may never show up on a stat sheet, it certainly helped to change the trajectory of my not-so-stellar football career.

Football, simply put, is about protecting the guy with the ball. This gives him the best chance to make a play, advance the ball, or maybe even score. On kickoffs, this involved coordinating the deep players of the receiving team. Their job was to follow the flight of the ball and align in a wedge formation in front of the return man. His job was to catch and run the ball back. Without overstating, it's not as easy as they make it look. I had improved my speed but not my running back skills. Maybe because of my improved speed, the coaches put me on the kickoff team and gave me a shot at this thing called wedge-buster. By name alone, you can probably guess what was expected of me. I remember Coach explaining it, in not so many words.

"Lewis, run fast, find the wedge, and crash into it."

This had a simplistic yet familiar feel to it. I thought back to my days playing rec league basketball. This wasn't going to be much different than finding the kid with the ball and fouling him. In fact, the way I saw it, this would be the perfect job for me. I had plenty of training as my team's designated fouler. In a weird way, I was proud of myself when I managed to foul out, despite most of my playing time occurring in the last few minutes of each game.

If this was my dad's football story, he would be able to recall the opponent, the final score, and how this play was a crucial part of a comeback victory. But it's my story, and honestly, I'm not even sure we won this game. It could be the cumulative effect of all my concussions. I do remember the ball in the air. I didn't think I could run this fast. In an instant, I was past the front line of defenders. Like a fighter pilot, the site lines formed by the bars of my face mask homed in on the center of the wedge.

Now, just a few feet from the wedge, I thought this collision might hurt. The feeling of making a tackle is sort of like being in a car wreck. There was a big clatter when our shoulder pads met, followed in the next half second by a loud whack when our helmets collided. I heard moaning but couldn't tell if it was him or me.

There was a suspended moment when our bodies were falling to the ground; it felt like it was happening in slow motion. It was just long enough to figure out I would land on him. It all sped up quickly but stopped with a jerk when our bodies bounced on the ground. I felt his gasp for breath and spray of spit on my face. The whistle blew and I knew it was safe to open my eyes.

I'd love to attribute what happened that day to some acquired skill, insightful coaching, or hours spent in a weight room. But I think, as the saying goes, I happened to run to the right spot, hit the right guy, at the right moment, and at the right angle. What showed up on film was nothing short of the first members of the wedge falling down like bowling pins. Apparently, I still had ahold of the guy I hit, and he kept going backwards. By sheer luck I drove him right into the helpless back he was supposed to protect. I had taken out the wedge and tackled the guy with the ball.

There was some cheering and my JV coaches were sure happy to see me on the sidelines. The play never caught the eye of a college recruiter or NFL scout. Much to my dismay, no college coaches would come to my high school asking about me. But one person did see the video of the play. The one person who mattered more than most others to me.

Thursdays are the last day of practice before most high schools light up their field for Friday night. It's also the day Coach Highfill would announce the JV players who earned the honor of dressing for the following night's varsity game. If you got to play your sport professionally or even at the college level, I recognize this may not mean much. For me, the freshman kid who hardly played a down, and the sophomore who just got lucky, this was a big deal.

The sun was waning, and Coach Highfill had blown his whistle. He started naming the guys who would dress. Hartsel, Butch, and Cunningham were always good bets to suit up. But this day he went on. He was at the end of his list and genuinely seemed to be struggling as he tried to remember if there was anyone else. And then the light went on. His head started to nod as he raised one finger and said, "Oh yeah, I almost forgot. The coaches told me I had to watch this one play from the JV game. This guy took out the entire wedge and made the tackle all in one play. That 'Mad Man' Lewis, I want you to dress tomorrow night."

There was a team breakdown, and those who weren't selected to dress left for the day. The rest of us stayed to run the two-minute drill, maybe review a new wrinkle in the offense, and hear a speech from Coach. I blindly hoped tomorrow's game would not come down to me being able to perform any of what was reviewed. I hadn't remembered much of anything else after Coach's announcement. I am sure I high-fived a few guys and I bet I anticipated sharing this news with Dad. But I only remembered my name being called and three simple words, "I want you ..."

●　　●　　●

I think there is a part in all of us who want to hear words like that spoken to us. Be it by someone picking teams on a playground, a pretty girl in junior high, or acknowledgment from a teacher or coach. Perhaps you loved pleasing your parents or maybe you waited for the call after the job interview. Who doesn't want to be chosen?

As much as I enjoyed hearing my name called by coach, he wasn't God. Why do we throw away so many chances to hear His voice call our name? More important than dressing for a varsity football game, each of us is continually invited and can hear our name being called. But we have to lose ourselves. We have to be quiet and be still.

Unfortunately, we fill our lives with a lot of technology and activity. Even good things like working out can easily take over our free time. We let social media or keeping up with the news distract us and take over portions of our lives that we might instead spend being quiet enough to hear the call. Sometimes it might mean an uncertain or different path than we had ever imagined ourselves traveling. Are you willing? Can you put down the phone, put down this book, find a quiet place, be still and listen?

Our Father calls out our name every moment of every day. The moments we take as our good luck, He makes a pathway. In the tougher times, it's hard to see, but He's there chipping away, using the experience to refine us. I had a pastor friend give me some great advice: "God is always with you. He's like a painter painting in a room full of doors and windows. We have total freedom to choose what we do. We can reach to open and close doors. Sometimes we get frustrated when a door doesn't open. We might even tug on it again and again."

Maybe like a sophomore wedge-buster, you've tried to break down more than one door. You forced your way through, only to find a tiger waiting to devour you. Maybe we check to see if there's a door or window. We like to have backup plans. We tell ourselves that any action is better than no action. But does our escape lead us to a green pasture, or a two-story drop? Maybe the best choice is to move. And sometimes, we can choose to just stand still. God is good with that. He can use all of those circumstances to paint over you and move along the piece of art He is making in you.

There is a song my dad loved to listen to called "Abba Father." The song uses the image of a potter using clay. If you've worked with clay, you know the process isn't always easy and frequently gets messy. Too often we can perceive a failed marriage or business as punishment. Sometimes we suffer through an addiction or disease, either our own, or that of a loved one. We question, How could a loving God allow this? There are no easy answers for the hard things in this world. But perhaps, when we return to the image of a potter working with the imperfections of clay, we can better understand. He's unafraid to add more water, not afraid to throw it back on the wheel to start over with us again. The skilled hand of the potter is able to work around the imperfections of the clay.

Maybe you prefer the idea of a painter painting a room—or on the grand canvas we call life. Our Father is unafraid to use the darker colors or uncertain background scenes to create great contrast and depth from a single dimension. Can you imagine being a painter when the subjects, the characters you created, have choice in what they do? Maybe it's a stretch, but it's the best way I can grasp what I think our Creator goes through.

He decided to give us choice. Some of us turn to friends or loved ones for support when things get difficult. Some are determined to go it alone and try to pull themselves up by the bootstraps. Still others find counseling, seek therapy, labeling people and behaviors as helpful ways to understand what's going on around them or in their relationships.

And of course, some choose to self-medicate with sex, drugs, and food, while some of us lean on shopping, social media, or anything else to numb the pain we feel. I am sure there are other manners in which people process things. I am not claiming to have a complete list. But regardless of what experts would add, I don't think it's how God intended things to be.

Sure, I suppose if you don't believe, you might see religion or God as just another way for people to self-medicate. I've been told more than once my faith is a crutch. I don't really know what happens when the last breath leaves my lungs. I know one day I'll find out. I also know all the things I've used to try and fill the void. I know all the ways I've tried to make sense of the crashing waves this world brings our way. Time and time again, it's the matters of faith that allowed me to stand.

A buddy of mine who doesn't believe, once described religions and faith by saying I'm attached to a big rock with gigantic rubber bands. And no matter how fast or far I run, I snap back to it. He thinks until I somehow cut those bands, I'll be doomed to repeat my trouble. I suppose that's one way to look at it. But by the same token, there is a sense of being anchored and united with something way bigger than me.

That day on the field, I was united with the coaches who'd seen the play and told Highfill about it. I was united with the guys who normally got to dress for varsity. I guess in a sense, I felt like I was united with my Dad too. The way I see faith is this: our Father is the rock we are connected to. He doesn't change and yet He gives us the total freedom to run away. Heck, we can even completely cut the bonds, if we are so inclined. But even then, like the father and his prodigal son, God stands waiting. He's looking out on the horizon for us to come home.

Have we had enough of trying things our own way? Had enough of the so-called friends who leave you when the party is over? Have we spent enough time sleeping in the pigpen, eating their slop? Maybe our relationship with our earthly father is part of what's messed up. That's a tough spot to be in, for sure. Be assured your heavenly Father still stands, waiting to welcome you back. He's called your name, and sees you as perfect and blameless, dressed in righteousness. He's got plans, tailor-made, just for you.

CHAPTER 19

Understanding the Assignment

What comes to mind when you hear the word teacher? Does it take you back to grade school? Do you have a family member or a friend who works with children? Perhaps your pastor comes to mind. There's also something known as the "School of Hard Knocks" or the "University of Real Life." Whether it's an experience, a person, or a mix of both, we all have those stories to tell when we learn something a little differently.

For me, it was my junior-year term paper. I don't remember the author I chose or the topic I presented. But I will never forget the instructor, Mr. Curtis Books. No, that's not his real name. I've changed it, but recalling his large stash of a particular book, it's an accurate description.

Maybe, like me, you made a special effort to be nice to your teachers. It's one of the first lessons we learned in school. We were supposed to be respectful to our teachers. Unfortunately, this would be one of the things I took a little too far. I lived to get others to like me. Sure, I was being respectful, but I would try to be extra friendly. I tried to learn about them and find something we had in common. And funny—oh, how I leaned on being funny. I worked hard for a well-timed joke for comic relief, just anything, because I wanted them to like me. I figured if I could make them smile or laugh, we were friends. I concluded it would be hard for a teacher to fail a student they liked.

I know now, I was thinking about this all wrong. But back then, I had spent years trying to get teachers and others to like me, and junior year would be no different. Old habits die hard, and this year, this teacher, was just the next one. I had to find a way to get him to like me. He was a unique man, for sure, a bit stuffy for juniors in high school. He was the quintessential English teacher with a head full of gray hair, always parted on the side. He wore black-rimmed glasses that I suppose could be seen as a throwback to the '50s. Back then I thought they were odd, but as I'm now in my fifties, I have a similar pair I use for my reading glasses.

No one ever made fun of him or called him Four Eyes. He would, on occasion, remove the glasses and place the bow in his mouth. It was a pause, while he gathered his thoughts. He had an incredible vocabulary full of words none of us knew. And that's saying something, because this was a college-bound class. Clearly increasing our vocabulary was high on his list of priorities.

He seasoned his lectures with fancy words and inevitably we all fell for it. He'd use a word we didn't know, and one of us ended up asking what it meant. When this happened there was a certain glimmer in his eye, and he stopped what he was doing. He victoriously pointed to the far side of the classroom, where his enormous bookshelf full of dictionaries sat. With the enthusiasm as if he'd discovered electricity, he'd smile and beam the word, "Dictionary!"

We all knew what this meant: a walk of shame to the bookcase, grabbing a dictionary, returning to stand by our desk, finding the word, and reading it aloud for the entire class. Rather than return it he told us to hold onto it, for the next word we didn't understand. His subtle Southern drawl came across almost as sophisticated as a British accent. For sure, he was a smart guy, but when I'd found out he, too, had been a wrestler when he was my age, I thought I had my in. This was a short-lived dream, as it became perfectly clear he would have nothing to do with my attempts to befriend him the day he called me "an incorrigible yahoo."

I made the mistake of responding, "Mr. Books, I don't know what that means, but I am pretty sure you just offended me."

His response? Say it with me—dictionary!

For those of you keeping score at home, incorrigible means incapable of being corrected or amended: not reformable, depraved, delinquent. A yahoo, not to be confused with a wahoo, is defined as a brute, or a boorish, crass stupid person. When I finished reading those definitions aloud, he simply said, "Hmmmmm. I'd say another accurate description. Well, thank you, Mr. Lewis."

At seventeen, the second zinger went right over my head. I was just happy he thought I had some muscle.

The day he announced the term paper assignment went something like this: "Ladies and gentlemen, this term paper will be graded on a curve. Despite the fact this is a college-bound class, none of you will earn an A, some of you may earn a B, but I doubt it. Most of you will deserve a C or D. And looking at the likes of this group, there will likely be some amongst you who will entirely fail to meet my requirements."

Being the seventeen-year-old, hopeless, bad beyond repair brute, I simply heard a triple-dog dare. Now I recognize this next statement may make me sound as curmudgeonly as my eleventh-grade English teacher, but it's true. The kids I work with these days have it entirely too easy. Nowadays students are graded on a

10-point scale, meaning an A was anything from 100 down to 90; B, was anything down to 80, and so on.

When I was a kid, we earned our A. Our grading scale was dramatically different:

100–95 = A
94–88 = B
87–81 = C
80–74 = D

Anything below a 74, well, you probably already know. There was also some fancy figuring around half points too. For example, a 94.4 was a B but a 94.5 or higher was typically rounded up to an A.

Looking back, it wouldn't take a Rhodes Scholar to realize how my grades would've benefited from today's scale. The next few English class periods, Mr. Books used an overhead projector. He hadn't used it all year, but for the next two weeks he would. Of course, for us to see the screen he'd have to turn off half the lights. And any self-respecting high school junior can tell you, this means one thing—nap time!

I don't think I actually fell asleep, but I wanted to. Mr. Books droned on and on—about which paper to use, what our table of contents should look like, how to make proper footnotes and number our pages. An entire day was devoted to the perils of plagiarism. He carried an air of genuine excitement when showing us how to create a formal works cited list. I wasn't entirely tuned out, but I was not taking as many notes as the smart kids.

● ● ●

I was, however, smart enough, or lucky enough, to be dating the girl who would eventually be our senior class yearbook editor. Now, I know what you are thinking: I, the jock, took advantage of the yearbook editor to read or flat-out write my term paper. While the thought did cross my mind, dating someone to do my work wasn't me. Plus, Mr. Books had made this personal when he made it clear no one would earn an A. Sure, I recognized the resource. I'm sure I talked about my ideas and maybe even had her read it.

She was a Baptist girl and with me being raised Catholic, we might as well have been members of the Jets and Sharks or Montagues and Capulets. I had watched members of my family live and express their faith. Now I had the chance to see others do so. On occasion I attended her church. It was different. Some things appealed to me more, other aspects less so. I felt like I was growing in my faith. And just like a baby bird discovers and flutters its wings, even when it doesn't know what wings do, I started to flutter mine. I'd go to church with my family and sometimes with hers. Privately, I thought of myself as a "Batholic."

It felt good to take some sense of ownership for this new part of my life. My family brought me up well. I knew to do my best to avoid trouble. Mom and Dad seemed supportive of this new relationship, but my grandmother was less certain. The fact I was dating a Baptist girl sure seemed to be one of those things she said would "make shame for the family." It seemed a waste of time to point out how in Southwest Virginia, it was mathematically less likely to find a "good Catholic" girl. Even though math wasn't my best subject, I did understand the concept of rounding numbers up or down. You ask what does all this have to do with a junior-year term paper and dating a Baptist girl? I'm not 100 percent sure myself, but I knew what it meant the day we got our term papers back.

Mr. Books was passing out our graded papers and unceremoniously dropped mine on my desk. It was a 94.4, rounded down to a B. It was the highest possible grade he could've given and still held to his word that none of us would earn an A. You'd think he might have said "Congratulations" or "Well done," but this was not Mr. Books. He mumbled some sort of comment under his breath, which I think implied I either got lucky or had help. He said, "Aberration." I didn't know what the word meant back then, but I knew better than to risk being sent to the dictionaries.

A similar scene played out again years later. I'd be back at the same school—this time as an assistant wrestling coach. I was attending college classes to complete my secondary teacher certification for, of all topics, English literature and language arts. I was entering the school a little later than normal, and just happened to enter as the hallways filled with students moving to their next class. I saw some of the wrestlers and waved hello, but then there he was, Mr. Books.

It was the first time I'd seen him, and I decided to say hello. I walked up to him and sort of reintroduced myself. To his credit, he recognized me. I wanted to share with him what I was doing. Maybe it was an attempt to let him know he'd inspired me in his own way. I enthusiastically told him how I was completing my studies and hoped to be an English teacher just like him. Mr. Books removed his glasses. There was a noticeable pause. No smile, more of a puzzled look on his face. For a moment, I thought he was going to go back and retroactively give me the A.

He said, "Mr. Lewis." Then another pause. "Good to see you making something of your life."

And with that, he turned and walked away. Yes, I was disappointed. I was hoping to convey how he'd motivated me or how he'd made a difference. Whether he acknowledged it in a way that made me feel good was not the point. I knew this much: like my coaches, Mr. Books had high standards.

Who knows, maybe his response was the best he could do in the moment. Perhaps he was concerned our brief conversation would make him late to his classroom. Maybe he'd never had a student come back to him to say thanks.

But the day we got our term papers back, it was less about making a teacher feel good. I didn't stand up and "spike" my paper as if it were a football. I knew better. Not just because I was a lineman and unlikely to ever score a touchdown. In part, my reaction came more from what coaches had drilled into me. And partly something

I'd somehow learned from Mr. Books: "Put in the work and let the rest of it come to you." And also: "It may not always work out the way you envision it, but don't be surprised when there's success." And most importantly, "Act like you've been there before."

That day I quietly took my 94.4 B, smiled a little, and scored one for the yahoos.

• • •

For those of us who've made it through the maze of navigating high school classrooms and romantic relationships, we know things can get confusing fast! It's easy to misinterpret a look, a comment, or the purpose of our assignment. But things don't get easier as we get older, especially when it comes to matters of faith. There are countless people we meet, but the number gets smaller when we consider who we allow to influence our life. For many, our list includes family, friends, teachers, and coaches. As we get older it might also include coworkers, bosses, or spouses. Still others are inspired by authors, musicians, or artists. You'd think the more people we have as examples, our path, our decisions, would be made easier. But we know it's not.

Most of us figure out how easy it is to get turned around when we are caught in the game of making others like us. It didn't work in high school, and it doesn't work now. I'm not suggesting having friends is a bad thing. I like discovering new influences, but maybe our definition, our understanding of the assignment is off. Do we fully understand the who, what, why, where, and when of our influences?

We invest so much time in comparison and contrast. As an English teacher, I thought this was a great tool, and I taught students to use it, as one way of stating their opinions. But as a believer, it can be our undoing. There is a phrase in the Bible that reminds us to run the race set before us. I think this sounds a lot like something my elementary school teachers would often say. Did you ever hear one of yours say, "Keep your eyes on your own paper"? If we spend our days focused on the circumstances, the possessions, the things which others have and what we don't, we are not running our race. I am not suggesting we live isolated, unconnected lives, but God has something planned for each of us. It might be a music career. Perhaps you will be one of the few who compete on a world stage. Or maybe you get to have a family, a spouse, or great friends to walk with. God is doing something uniquely designed for you to make Him known. Let's stay focused on our race.

I never was good with numbers, and I never did get the tenth of a point from Mr. Books, and that's OK. For those intrigued by numbers and looking to refocus on the race before them, love is never a bad place to start. We know it's less about dating the yearbook editor. We don't need to be friends with our English teacher. We just need to focus on the Teacher. Jesus mentions loving each other at least fourteen times in the New Testament. I think this makes loving each other the perfect starting point.

CHAPTER 20

A Tree of Life

My teenage identity angst was consuming me. Despite all the workouts, despite going to church, playing sports, trying to be a good student, a good kid, and to not "make shame for the family," privately I was sinking deeper into confusion and despair. Despite hearing the voice at the Weekend of Champions, despite a family and parents who loved me the best they could, despite the gift of great coaches, teachers, and friends who liked me, I was fighting a losing battle. "Despite being born with a large head and trying to laugh off the resulting names from the neighbor kids like "The Wad" and "Watermelon Head," despite trying to play along with hurtful, projected names from a sibling, despite having a girlfriend or two and athletic successes, it wasn't enough to quiet my doubts about myself and the feeling that I didn't fit in. My emotional confusion was consuming me."

Publicly all I knew was to keep up the happy facade. Keep making people like you, keep making people laugh, and it will all be OK. But alone in the dark, I couldn't quiet the despair that my family didn't like me and wouldn't stick up for me. My doubts and despair had convinced me that nothing I could do would ever be right, that I should quit fighting and give in to its demands. And maybe like yours, despite all the pressure, the promise, the hope of peace and fulfillment, my confusion and despair kept lying to me. Every time I gave in, it left me feeling empty, dirty, wrong, unwanted, unlovable, and unfixable. It didn't matter what the priest or preacher said. Nothing my coaches or teachers ever taught me seemed to help fight it off.

I'd spent many nights white knuckling it, crying, pleading, begging for clarity. God, if you are there, take it away from me, change me to what the voices are telling me or please take me home. The pain, the confusion is too much for me to bear. All of the bravado failed, prayers failed. My confusion was destroying me. The years of trying to get family, friends, teachers, and coaches to like me had exhausted me. The weight of going it alone was crushing me. The thought of carrying this burden the rest of my life was overwhelming and I wanted this all to be over.

My parents were out of town again, family was all gone, I was home alone, and this was my chance. I was tired of being the good kid, the one who tried to follow rules, tried to keep the peace. I tried going to two different churches and FCA, but it all seemed to fail me. All of my effort fell short. Despite some success athletically and with the term paper, the early voices of self-doubt kept shouting their message—that no matter what I did, it wasn't enough, that I wasn't enough. It didn't matter how hard I fought or how many times I started over again, my despair was consuming me. The voice in my head echoed, This is the only way out.

I looked at the label and discovered they'd been prescribed to our dog who had died. It was a big bottle, so I figured even if this stuff was old, this many should do it. I opened the pill container and poured the pills into my hand. As they poured out, a chalk-like powder fell, covering my hand like a small dusting of flour. I held all of them in my hand and even though my mom said I was great at taking pills, I knew I couldn't possibly swallow this many without something to drink. I didn't want to chicken out. Then I remembered the wine cooler in the fridge. Dad always joked about beer being as refreshing as horse pee. So this was the closest thing to alcohol we had. Lower your inhibitions and swallow them all. This was my plan as I sat in the kitchen near the counter island.

I looked down at the pills and over at the wine cooler. I thought about my parents and sisters coming home and finding me. I didn't care. My despair was consuming me, and this was how I could win. Out of the corner of my eye, I saw the extra-long phone cord we had attached to our phone. The phone attached to the wall. My parents had gotten the cord so they could easily move about the kitchen while still taking a call. It came in handy when we wanted a private conversation too: we could walk the phone into another room. Because it was so long, it easily tangled up. And that's what caught my eye. The long curly cord, curled upon itself. I'd seen my parents unplug the cord from the base unit. Then they would hold the cord high and allow the phone handle to spin freely and untangle the cord. I thought, If they are going to find me, I could at least untangle the phone cord. I put the pills and drink down and proceeded to repeat what I'd seen them do. It was my last try to do something right. The phone was done spinning and I plugged it back in the base. The instant hum of the open line was inviting me to place a call. Just then I remembered the pills and the drink but as I got ready to turn back to them there it was: Coach Trent's handwritten phone tree. It stopped me.

I wondered if this list would be used to notify the team of what I'd done. Would anyone bother to show up at my funeral, like when two of our friends died in a car crash? The voices told me no, and I believed they were right. But it was Coach's handwriting. This was the guy who took a chance on me and asked me to be on his varsity team my freshman year. It was Coach who had invited me to the weekend where I heard the voice. Something told me I owed him something.

My despair was consuming me, and I wanted it to end, but like a prisoner with one call, I decided to make mine. I knew I couldn't call Coach. The thoughts in my head convinced me he'd be mad, disappointed, and even angry he'd tried to help. My eyes looked up and down the list. And I came across Trae's name.

I think I picked him because we played together on the defensive side of the ball. I was the noseguard, and he was the tackle. He was a year ahead of me and I looked up to him. When our coaches moved me to noseguard, I was undersized, and I knew it. It was Trae who took me under his wing. I had to call the defensive huddle every play and I remember Trae telling me to "call it like you mean it." He gave me a voice and I really looked up to him. And then it was wrestling season.

I'd felt badly because Coach Trent would ask me to wrestle at 155 pounds. My first thought was, This is a great idea, my natural weight. That was until I realized I'd have to wrestle off against Trae. He was a senior but a first-year wrestler. He was strong, fast, and playing alongside of him for football, I'd seen how downright mean he could be in competition. I didn't like my odds.

Wrestle-offs were best two out of three. I can't remember the first two matches. But I remember the day it was all even, we'd each won one, and today it would be decided. The whole team was jogging on the outside of the mat. Coach Trent would officiate, and he called us to the middle. Most of the older guys were cheering for Trae. Heck, part of me was cheering for Trae. But I beat him. I was happy, sad, and fearful he was going to beat the crap out of me. We shook hands and I was the starter.

Maybe this is why I picked Trae's name. I figured he'd be pissed, probably wouldn't answer the call, and I'd have my answer.

To my surprise, he did pick up. It was late when he asked, "What's up?"

I sputtered my words as I told him I was home alone, and I didn't want to live anymore. That was easier than explaining everything. Trae said and did all the right things. He wasn't that pissed-off guy I thought he would be for taking his spot. He was the guy who took me under his wing. I told him where I lived, and he drove over to my house. I really don't recall exactly what was said or even how long he stayed. I do remember he flushed the pills and wine cooler down the toilet; he even made sure I didn't have any other pills or alcohol. Eventually he got ready to leave. I begged him not to tell anyone. But of course, he did. He told the right person.

● ● ●

Ms. Stone was our geometry teacher and yes, she was married to my elementary school principal. She was a little older, but did well with our rowdy bunch. Her lessons were well thought out, and she was happy when we got excited about how this math actually showed up in the real world.

She was surprised by a knock at her classroom door. She opened the door and then I was equally surprised. I sat up a little straighter than normal. It was Coach Highfill.

He asked her if he could borrow me for a little while. She was puzzled and so was I. Coach didn't say much as we walked down the hallway. He just said, "Let's wait 'til we get outside."

This was fine by me, but now my mind had time to race through all the possibilities. Optimistically, I wondered if maybe some small college coach was asking about me. Then I wondered if something had happened to my parents and the school had sent Coach to break the news. I quickly dismissed those notions. I carefully went through all my other classes and teachers trying to recall if I had said or done something or maybe forgotten an assignment. Each teacher, each class went through my mind. Was I current on all my homework? I didn't get to the answer before we made it outside and he asked, "What's up bud?"

I remembered this was close to the way Trae had answered the phone the other night. I mumbled, "Not much."

There was a long pause and then he asked, "Are you feeling all right?"

It occurred to me, maybe during our walk in the hall, Coach was also searching his brain for the right words to say. He added, "I heard you might've been having a little trouble and I wanted to see if I could help."

I realized then that Trae had told Coach about the other night. I wasn't mad at Trae. In fact, I was kinda relieved he had said something, even more relieved that he'd told the man I was walking alongside.

I was suddenly even more grateful for this man I'd only met because I wanted to get out of a class back in eighth grade. Coach was a man I really looked up to, a man who built a program within which his players could trust him. We knew Coach wanted to make us better players ... but more importantly, better men. There was more Coach and I talked about during our walk, but these were two things I knew from that day forward. One, I had better choices than old dog pills and a wine cooler. I had coaches and teammates who genuinely cared. And two, sometimes a phone tree has an entirely different use than was ever intended. Perhaps the same can be said for regular trees too. We see them as green, lush, full of leaves. But there's so much more.

● ● ●

Trees are pretty incredible. They give us things like paper, provide shade, even a place for birds to build a nest and a place for squirrels to scamper. Trees give us life as they change our exhaled carbon dioxide into fresh oxygen. And it was a tree cut down for the purpose of Jesus' crucifixion that truly gave us life. It's easy to say we'd do something for whatever we consider a noble purpose. I've said it myself about a variety of things. But few of us actually would. At least not without creating a social media post, getting recognition, or earning a tax credit. There was one man who did, though, and not too many people debate His existence or His horrific manner of death.

The Old Testament foreshadows it and the Gospels spell it out graphically. They say He died for our sins, for our moments of less than, for our childhood deceptions and our grown-up lies. He saw it all. He saw mine and yours. He has seen what we've done and what we're going to do. He knows about the time we wanted to end it all, the time we were little and told a little lie. He knows the bigger one we told someone else and the biggest ones we keep telling ourselves.

But He's not the mean nun or Sunday school teacher lording it over you. Because He's also seen what's been done to you. By the parent, the spouse, the mean little kid in the third grade, the boy or girl who broke your heart. He saw the family friend or the evil stranger who touched and did unspeakable things to you. He saw what was done to them as well.

He came to teach us many things, but the greatest two were pretty simple. "Love God" and "love our neighbors the same as we love ourselves." While doing so, He saw our mistakes. And even though He didn't do the things we've done to each other, He knew His next step. His actions that Friday said it all. He paid the price on the tree. He chose death to give us life.

There were those who wept. Those He came back and visited. There were those who were glad He died and was no longer a threat to them. There were those who probed fingers into His wounds and believed, and those who still refused Him. He came to live among us and show us what is good. In return, He wants us to do three things: to act justly, love mercy, and walk humbly with our God. When will we recognize that our actions and words have the power of life and death? Even the ones we think are small and simple. One coach wrote out a phone tree. Trae answered a phone call. And another coach pulled a kid out of class to take a walk and talk things out.

I am not saying God ignores or doesn't see our shortcomings, our addictions, our problems, our failures. Just the opposite. He saw it all and took action: He took the next step and sent His Son to us. Jesus chose death so that we could have life. He's not worried about what you've done, what's been done to you, or what you say you are going to do next. He sees past it all and cares about just one thing: our response to His love today.

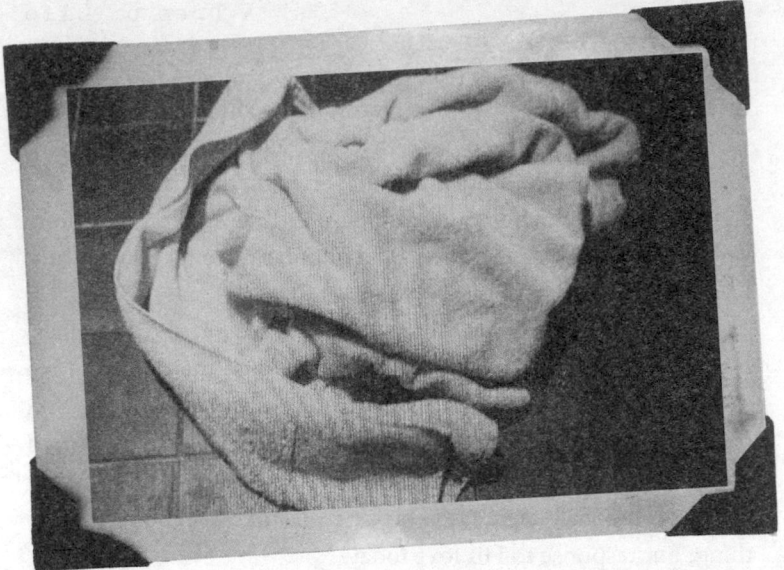

CHAPTER 21

Don't Leave Grace on the Floor

It's funny how things can look one way and turn out another. You wouldn't have been able to guess my freshman year that I'd even stick with football. Senior year, things really came together for me. As our three-a-day practices began early one August morning, some things remained the same. Players from years past showed up to watch. The current players put on helmets and cleats; at the first practices, we didn't wear full pads. It occurred to me I was a senior, and while there was hope some college would ask me to play for them, this would be the last, first day, here.

The smell of freshly cut grass and the sounds of an optimistic group of boys filled the air. The younger guys had their names written on athletic tape. New players had to wear it across the front of their helmets, so coaches could learn their names. Before practice started, I recalled each step of my journey. From the eighth grader just getting out of a class to the freshman who barely played at all. Sophomore year was the play on kickoff that let me dress for a varsity game. Junior year had the move from the backfield to lineman, even getting to start on defense. This year we had an experienced group of twenty-three seniors and every reason to be fired up.

In our part of the state, twenty-three seniors was a big group. We had set a team goal of winning the district championship, something no one in our group had ever seen done. During off-season workouts, I was humbled to be nominated and selected by teammates to serve as a captain. Maybe I wasn't going to play at the college level but being selected as a captain would be something to share with Dad. If we won the championship, it would be another shared experience. The whistle blew and the first day of the final year of practice started. The first week came and went, but ended with a warning.

Coach said there were far too many towels being left on the floor as we showered after each practice. He and the other coaches weren't our mommas, he said, and they weren't going to be picking them up. On one hand I thought, Towels? We are trying to win a championship and he's talking to us about towels? I didn't see a connection, but Coach had my attention. He would give us a chance to fix it now, on our own, or he'd let us have time to think about towels during a nice long run in full pads. I'd like to say it was a sense of responsibility or perhaps an act of leadership when I just started staying later and making sure each guy put his towel in the appropriate basket. The truth is, the moment Coach uttered the word run, I flashed back to my track and field experiment. Those practices were held on the track surrounding our game field. The very track on which I'd earned, and returned, my team sweats. I was determined the scene would not be repeated. Even if it meant I confronted a guy or two.

I don't know how many towels were ever left out. In hindsight, maybe it was just a foreshadowing of Coach kicking us out of practice the next week. By this time, the older guys had at least seen this before. Coach had sent everyone home in previous seasons. But this seemed different. Our practice had begun with a lack of effort. Maybe it was a cumulative result of wearing full pads and collisions. It could've been the increased mental and physical workload of three practices a day, or maybe it was the heat. But from the beginning of practice, our coaches were on us for dragging.

Eventually Coach blew his whistle and called us all in. It didn't take much to realize this huddle up was different. The normally calm, cool, and collected Coach Highfill removed his sunglasses, raised the brim of his ball cap, and placed his hands together as if praying. The hands were placed in just the right spot so that Coach's index finger touched his lips. Any one of these nonverbal cues could be interpreted multiple ways. By themselves, they could lead to something good. But for those of us who'd been around, we knew when these gestures were done together it wasn't a good sign.

Coach wasn't one to cuss or swear, but he let us know when our performance was not cutting it. He said we weren't practicing up to our abilities, that this was unacceptable, and was not going to help us accomplish our goals or have a successful season. He sent us all off the field. He provided a set amount of time to run back, hang up our gear, and get out of the locker room. He said he didn't want to see a single person's face—and we knew there better not be a helmet out of place or a single towel on the floor. We were all gone well before the allotted time expired.

We'd been dismissed before nine a.m. and disappeared per Coach's direction, but I returned well in advance of our midday special-teams practice. I carefully snuck into the locker room. As silently as possible I opened my locker to gather my cleats and quietly closed it. I proceeded to the cage in socks to avoid detection, put on my full gear, and slipped out the door. I went up the hill, past the stadium and stood by the locked gate leading to our practice field. I just stood like a caged bull, ready to buck.

As most adolescent young men do, I had internalized and personalized Coach's message. I felt as a leader I hadn't done my part. It was my fault we weren't performing as we should. My mission by the gate was to be the final checkpoint for every player before they entered afternoon practice. It would be a good one.

Now this all sounds well and good around 10:30 a.m. It was at least a little cooler than it would be for midday practice. With my helmet and chinstrap buckled, I waited in the sun. I continued to wait as it got hotter and hotter. Eventually sweat started to bead and come down my neck and face. Some slipped into my eyes, and it burned. But by this point not much of what I had was dry. Upon closer inspection, I discovered the gate leading to our practice field was unlocked. The heat was getting to me and the stairs leading down the hill seemed to be offering the chance to sit. The sun and the temperature rose. While sitting on the top stair I laid back and closed my eyes.

What on earth was I thinking? Practice wouldn't start for another hour, and I was whupped from the heat. I don't know how much time passed, but I suddenly heard a voice I recognized. I opened my eyes and there, looking over me, was Coach asking if I was OK. Embarrassed I had dozed off, I stammered something about mentally getting ready for practice. He either believed me or was just relieved I wasn't out cold. I stood up as he walked over to the track surrounding our game field and proceeded to run. What on earth is he doing? I thought. Here it was the hottest part of the day, so hot it had put me to sleep. And he chose this time to run?

It spoke volumes. It was clear he was going to run whether I was there or not. There were no other coaches, no players, no one else around. The fact he delayed his run and came over to check on the idiot who'd dressed in full gear two hours before practice, said more about him than me. I kept trying to wrap my head around the why. Why would Coach run before practice? He didn't have anything to prove. He wasn't a team captain or vying for a starting position. I'd contemplate the answers to those questions, but I would remain by the gate, even more determined to set the tone for a good practice. Still, negative thoughts found their way in.

I thought about the early practice when I had ignored a blocking assignment.

●   ●   ●

A whistle had blown, and Coach called me over. Understand by this time in my life, I was at least equally concerned about disappointing my coaches as I was my parents. Now face-to-face, Coach lifted the brim of his ball cap and looked over the top of his shades. He gently grasped my face mask. I'd seen Coach passionately make a point before. I'd seen him upset when he felt we had underperformed. But in four years I'd never seen him physically hurt anyone. I don't know why, but I was fearful I was going to be his first.

As I watched his fingers grasp my mask, my neck muscles tightened, anticipating a sudden jerk to remove my helmet, or worse, my head. He simply looked me in the eye and gently said, "We're clear that won't ever happen again, right?" I swallowed hard and said, "Yes, sir." Coach's fingers fell from my mask, he tapped me on the top of my helmet and said, "All right then, let's go to work." In hindsight, I don't know what I was really worried about. This was the man who pulled me out of class for a walk. This conversation was just another example of Coach's grace and compassion. But as someone who was new to receiving grace, I was like Bambi on ice, still growing, still figuring things out.

I don't recall the next play we ran; in fact, I was just happy to have not messed something up. All I could think about was the juxtaposition. I was fully accepting and understanding one thing, but Coach had given me the exact opposite. Back then I didn't have words or life experience to understand it. Just like my pop-pop had every right to be upset with my dad for breaking the window, Coach had every right to be upset with me. But instead, he offered grace.

• • •

Isn't this what our Father is offering us each and every time we mess up?

Grace is offered—to the doubting Thomas, to the tired fisherman who don't want to cast their nets again. It was given to Saul and to both a crowd holding stones and the woman who was their target. It was poured out of an earthen vessel to the other woman, the one by the well. It's waiting for the prodigal son (or daughter), for the one sheep who wanders off, and for a tax collector to climb out of a tree. It was exhaled for the convicted murderer hanging on the cross next to him as Jesus was about to breathe his last, it hangs for the daughter (or son) of an alcoholic, it's there for you ... and me, the seventeen-year-old football player.

Having faith and growing in grace are two of those things that can be hard to understand. Some say you have to accept grace in order to come to faith. Others insist it's only by faith you can understand grace. To me it all seems like a meaningless debate, sort of like which came first, the chicken or the egg? Grace is always there, just waiting to be used. When I played football, I thought building my muscles, impressing coaches, and getting to play in college like my dad was the ultimate goal. I didn't connect the dots until much later, but I think those workouts on the bench my parents had given me were all about earning it. I wanted to earn my parents' respect. I wanted my teammates and teachers to be proud of the person I was. And my coaches, oh, how I wanted to earn their respect.

Here in the middle of life, I look back to what I believed and valued. It all seems a little silly now. There's nothing wrong with a teenager going all in on sports. There's nothing wrong with trying to emulate and impress your parents or coaches. But here's the thing: sort of like God's grace, most parents are already in your corner. Coaches might challenge you and even occasionally get really upset about random things like towels being left out, but coaches and teachers also see the fire, commitment, and desire to do well. And like our parents, they are rooting for us, trying to help us maximize our effort.

Now here's the funny thing: faith and grace are the same but different. We make the mistake all too often of thinking we're coming to Jesus or doing something for God. The reality is, He's the one working on us. Sure, He's got things He'd prefer we do. I am quite certain there are choices He'd like us to make. But His work is not dependent upon what we do or choose. God is faithfully at work and His grace is always there for us to pick up the "towels" we left out and allows us to keep moving forward. Eventually we see ourselves growing in grace and faith. Maybe you look at faith and grace like coaches do football players. We sometimes start off for one reason. We think we have discovered a cool way of getting out of class, but in reality, we are starting a journey. One that will afford us the opportunity to build our muscles of faith and grace. We have the chance to grow and experience some life-changing relationships. We have a chance at winning the ultimate championship at Our Father's home field. Regardless of the sport or activity we've experienced, Jesus showed us the playbook and He used a towel that maybe was left out.

It was after dinner with His friends. He knew His season here was almost over. His mission was almost complete, the end was near. Rather than hoisting a trophy over His head, He took on the role of servant. Having dressed himself in just a towel, he took a bowl of water and washed their feet, in an act of service and love for them. One at a time, He connected with them. He looked at them and into their hearts. He thanked them and He loved them as He washed their feet. We know our time here won't be easy. At times it will seem like wave after wave of struggle, like winning is always beyond our grasp. But I don't think our purpose is about hoisting trophies or the titles we win. It's more about who we touch and how we serve them.

•   •   •

One by one the players showed up to practice. I started in on the first one and said something macho like, "You'd better buckle that helmet up tight." Soon we all were gathered. Almost without words, we agreed it was going to be a great practice. We worked ourselves into a frothy mess of sweat, adrenaline, and testosterone. Coaches arrived without a word to us, and that was fine. We just grew louder and louder, cheering each other on, anticipating the blow of the whistle and beginning of practice, our chance at redemption. It was a great practice. There were some hard hits and epic plays. Our coaches fed off our enthusiasm. It led to a good season.

Oh, and the championship—it came down to the final week. We were winning late in the game against our rivals, the Golden Eagles. If we won, technically it would put us in first place for the moment. But in the very next moment came the sound of the final horn, which ended our playing days for most of us. We walked off the field together, one more time, me and my brothers. We walked into the locker room knowing we had done all we could. But for it to hold up, the Cavaliers, a team we'd beat, would have to win over Alleghany. The Alleghany team had come to our house and had thoroughly pounded us, winning forty-two to nine. We didn't like our chances. But sort of like faith and grace, it's funny how things can look one way and turn out another. Those Cavaliers did end up pulling out the win and securing our team championship. We were excited to win and accomplish our goal. Here we saw ourselves on the mountaintop. We hadn't realized we were just starting our journey on the road to growing in faith and grace. We hadn't yet seen the lessons learned from a towel left out.

CHAPTER 22

The Clarion Call

Every town has attractions. It could be a place you should go to, or things they want you to see and do. Most towns have distractions too. The place or the history they don't readily talk about. Oddly enough, everyone knows about it, and like a magnet most are drawn to it. Clarion, Pennsylvania, was no different.

The dream of playing in the NFL was firmly behind, but my first year of college was front and center as my next step. The idea of wrestling at college was still flickering in the back of my mind. I thought maybe I could "walk on" for the team. I didn't know how quickly the idea would fade but I did know my future was a seven-hour drive away from all the familiar guardrails. There was no off-season lifting program, no wrestling tournaments. This was going to be a chance to try something new, to start a different journey. I was still wrestling my personal struggles and didn't know I was about to wrestle another, far stronger foe.

Items to be left behind were packed away, while certain must-haves were packed up. The Farrah Fawcett poster topped the list. Farewells and goodbyes were behind the day we started up I-81 North. It was just like all the trips back to Quakertown. But this time we'd alter the journey to ensure arrival at exit 64 off I-80 in western Pennsylvania.

Like so many freshman families, we made multiple trips up and down the hot, crowded staircase. We carried what would be my new life into room 309-A of Campbell Hall. None of us will forget the large bag of white powder my roommate had left on his desk chair. We still laugh nowadays remembering how relieved my parents were to learn it was foot powder and not anything else. We walked downstairs to our van one last time. We had eaten and gone through every possible extension of time together. Dad shook my hand and pulled me in for a hug as Mom put her purse in the front seat.

The woman I had butted heads with for most of my teenage years was also the woman who carried me for nine months. She closed the van door and turned back to me. Gone were disappointing looks and lectures about not trying my best. Her hands were coming to hold my head one more time, and she was in tears. I was, after all, her only boy. The boy who wrote his name on the wall of her new house. The boy who randomly added paint to her handmade Christmas ornaments. The boy who spooned out half the fruit filling from a pie she'd made. Her only evidence was a pink crust. The boy who played and hid in a tree outside her kitchen window was now the young man she would leave behind.

● ● ●

Clarion University wasn't the party school, but maybe a not-so-distant second. As if girls and new freedom weren't enough distraction, two others topped the list. The first was an eight hundred-forty-five-foot abandoned train trestle. They say work on the rail began in 1897, with a major overhaul in the late 1920s. The lines used to haul lumber from the area also made Clarion a destination. However, with the lumber gone, the line saw less traffic. The town wouldn't pay for the necessary updates and in the 1980s, the line was abandoned. Rails that had allowed countless trains and trees to roll away were pulled up and used somewhere else. This left behind the old, abandoned trestle.

At its highest point, the Clarion Trestle is an awesome twenty-one stories high. What remains today points to the impressive construction. There's a tunnel on each side of the trestle. One is constantly flooded, the other redecorated with colorful graffiti artwork. Once you enter the darkness of what's called Tunnel Three, your eyes are drawn 1,762 feet to the light at the end of it. Just beyond the exit, you stand on the edge of the enormous span. Gigantic steel bents are held in place by thick metal pins. The longest span is an impressive 270 feet long, all anchored into thick concrete, bearing a pour date of 1928.

The trestle was originally constructed to hold two lines. Some say humanity has two lines too. My grandmother said, "There are two kinds of people. Those trying to get to heaven and those on the Hell Express." I think she was both right and wrong. You can call her a liar if you want. But lying and falsely calling someone a liar are both items that could place someone on the latter train.

Philosophers say we grow wiser with age. I don't know if this is entirely true, but we sure do have more experiences to draw upon. Perhaps humanity is on two rails. For sure there are those who only see black or white, right or wrong, my way or no way. But most of us have concluded there are not only shades of gray, but incredible hues of color in the work of God. Trusting the work of the Creator, we assign different names for the two rails. Those who've seen more than two colors, two sides, and those on their journey to experience the same.

The other Clarion legend was Cry Baby Cemetery, an oddly shaped, well-manicured clearing off Triangle Road. Our college newspaper, The Clarion Call, offered up all sorts of information for incoming students, and I may have come across it here. According to locals, a wave of fever swept through the area in the late 1930s, claiming the lives of hundreds of children. Two of its victims, twin babies, were buried at Cry Baby Cemetery. However, they are at either end of the cemetery instead of next to each other. If you go out there at night, they say, you hear the twins cry out for each other.

●   ●   ●

A different fever sweeps through every college town in the Fall as students return to campus. Distractions cry out. Some won't fall for them, but many will. Our president told us our ability to focus on studies was a matter of life or death. He ominously instructed us to look to our left and right. He went on to say one of those people, or possibly you, will be gone by the end of spring semester. His point? One in three college freshmen drop out and never finish their college journey. I was almost the one.

College is like any other fork in the road of major life change. We can trust our experiences of seeing more than black or white. But life changes and faith present us with a duality of sorts. We know God loves us and is always there in the life or death of any cemetery we find ourselves. We know God is bigger than any trestle or journey we take. Yet God leaves us in charge of conducting our choices.

Despite the occasional adventure, I'd spent my life trying to be the good kid. But with the constant guidance from the rails of parents, sport, and coaches now removed, it was easy to get off track. We don't plan it, nor did I recall packing my emotional struggle. But sure enough, deep in the dark tunnel of myself, it was there. All previous attempts to free myself had failed. We tend to return to what we know. I buried myself in university life and getting people to like me.

I jumped into every aspect of college—except schoolwork. I replaced sports with broadcasting. My ability to fit in and get others to like me seemed to be an asset on campus. I was able to crack a starting lineup of sorts and enjoyed being a part of sports broadcasts. The dream of wrestling ended in one sense but opened another door. The walk-on opportunity wasn't pursued, but knowledge of the sport was put to work. I convinced the station manager, our television advisor, and the coach to broadcast our home wrestling matches. Clarion wrestled at the highest division and had national contenders on the team. The experience of the sport helped each broadcast and led to more opportunities.

It's funny how God never forces us to make decisions, choosing instead to work all things out. So often we can pause, look back over our life and see connections between seemingly random events. It's God pointing out His faithfulness, showing us the road map to life. God isn't in a panic over our wrong turns and paths through dark places. He is somehow always on the other side of the tunnel, leading us out. We don't have this kind of insight at eighteen. But even then, I tried to connect the dots.

I thought: childhood illnesses led me to Dr. Myer. He was the one who suggested to my mother that I consider wrestling. Wrestling had led to Coach Trent. Years of practices with Coach led to Clarion and this opportunity. Bitten by the broadcasting bug, a new dream emerged. It seems silly now, but then I believed I was put on the earth to replace Bob Costas on NBC's Olympic coverage. I know: a not-so-normal conclusion. But back then I was at a spot we often find ourselves in—needing a new dream. More time at the television and radio stations earned a spot on the sports talk call-in show and occasionally hosting the college's version of SportsCenter. Soon came an opportunity for on-air spots hosting our local high school and university football coverage. Everything was progressing ... except my grades.

My hallmates made fun of me for having a D in Human Sexuality. I thought I'd never live their ribbing down. In college you can drop a class to save your GPA; even so, after that first semester I was barely above a 2.0 GPA and sinking back into my private struggles. I started to drink heavily, pouring myself into drinking with the same ferocity I had poured myself into working out years earlier. Some of the upper classmates in the department were impressed, but drinking didn't help matters. There is more than one evening not remembered. The ones recalled are embarrassing.

I stood on couches and tables to sing along with every lyric as songs played. Lost in a jungle of emotions, self-pity, and a large dose of wanting to fit in, I was alone. I just wanted to be loved, really loved, by someone, anyone. Caught between being an on-camera star, making myself likeable, and the truth, I most often just wanted to be alone.

Dad had taught me a spoon-flipping trick he'd learned at the Naval Academy, and I was pretty good at it. After a few hours of trying to fit in by drinking with friends, I resorted to isolating for the rest of the party. I spent the rest of the evening, alone in a corner attempting to flip a butter knife into a longneck bottle as I drank. It never went in. Walking home I was stumbling, cold, and alone. It was a minor miracle campus police hadn't taken in this empty shell of a human being attempting to get back to his dorm. This is how drinking and losing to the demons left me: small, powerless, a shadow of the person I dreamed of becoming. Most of the time I looked good to others on the outside. Inside I was alone, scared, and surrounded by dark nothingness.

Drinking and the emotional confusion and despair I kept secret, continued to overwhelm. To explain, my attempt to cope was like eating something you love, except it's not food. It was like eating a blanket. Eyes gaze upon the beautiful blanket. It appears perfectly harmless. It promises comfort and warmth. It seems big enough to wrap ourselves up in it completely. We tuck ourselves in and listen to lies promising safety and protection from anything that could hurt. It sounds like an odd example, but fighting with demons will make a person imagine weird correlations.

When the very thing that comforts you, suggests such good things, you make decisions that otherwise don't make sense. At some point it envelops you and no longer brings the comfort or warmth you once thought it would. We keep taking it in but discover what was full of warm and fuzzy comfort actually contains shards of glass, each one further isolating and cutting us as consumed. We are left feeling more pain, more hurt, more alone, and more shame than before.

It's not all bad, all the time. Life in mental confusion can offer peaceful respites. Sort of like sitting under the trestle along the Clarion River. Hours and sometimes days of clarity can pass. There are normal bends in interactions and spots of smooth calm, commitments to do things right. But these don't always last. Around the bend, rapids return.

●   ●   ●

Real change happens down deep. Deeper than a six-foot grave at Cry Baby Cemetery and deeper than any river. The morning after giving away my virginity there was just such a moment. Trying to be a gentleman, I walked her back to where she was staying.

Some call it the walk of shame. Maybe they felt shame because she wasn't as pretty as they thought the night before. I felt shame because this wasn't me. I made my way home and had the moment in the mirror. Looking deep within I saw myself. In an instant I was physically there, but also not. Anchored deep inside were the memory and voice of a coach saying something about our effort. How even when we lost, if we could look ourselves in the mirror and truthfully answer we had done everything we could, he was good with that. The person looking back in the mirror couldn't answer those questions.

The next week I happened upon a poster inviting the reader to a Fellowship of Christian Athletes meeting. Recalling too many nights praying to a porcelain god and making empty promises to not drink again if I "just survived," I figured I should go. I did. It felt awkward, familiar, and right at the same time. Questions came: "If these people knew what I've been doing for months, would they allow me to stay or send me away?" Something deeper helped me see these were genuine people, the kind of person I wanted to be more like. Still the thoughts echoed: "These people have never even thought of the very things I have done."

One of the guys I met was a local. His parents lived nearby, and his dad shared his story. He had known the things I'd done, and even more. The Bible says a cord of two or three strands is not easily broken. I hadn't found these two or three guys—God had been conducting, working farther down the rail, and the train pulled into this station. Not surprisingly, most things turned around. However, there were new conflicts, like how to worship.

After church with my new friends, we'd return to campus. Just a few steps down and on the same side of the street, we'd pass the Catholic church. Something called to me as we walked by. I suspected my parents would've felt better if I'd gone there. I knew my grandmother would've, for sure. In truth, there were times I did sneak in by myself. It was there God taught me certain things. There in the silence God held a master class.

I'd light a candle. Sometimes I had a dollar to slip into the slot, other times I didn't. I am pretty sure the prayers counted and were heard either way. Often, I would be alone in the church. I'd sing the songs that made my Dad cry. The church had great acoustics. Good enough to make an average singer think they sound OK. But mainly there were silent conversations. I tried to talk to this

God and tried to understand things. I'd talk about everything from grades, to college, my frustrations, my hopes, and even the thorns in my side. Most of the time I'd sit quietly, desperately wanting to hear something back, but didn't. I wondered about that voice from years ago. Where was it now? It seemed like a one-way conversation.

Isn't this how life works? The Bible never says life will be without trouble. If anything, it assures us our journey will have struggles. Maybe, like me, you've tried all life has to offer, and maybe you, too, discovered none of it works. But by pressing in we can find answers—even in silence.

At any moment and any place, we can be still. We can commune with God. It may seem like a one-way conversation. Maybe we don't hear what is whispered to our heart. Maybe we connect the dots much later. We can come to appreciate our struggles as much as our time with Him. We aren't made to be alone. The addictions, the struggles, the loss, the hurts, are still real and will seem to isolate us. But we can also see these serve a higher purpose. We won't know some answers on this side, but we can know God is the good conductor. He built the biggest trestle, one that allows us to cross over, out of any cemetery we've chosen, just so we can be with Him. Hmmm, maybe the conversations weren't so one-way after all.

CHAPTER 23

Music to Our Heart

Nashville was my Nazareth. We all have a city associated with the time and place we start to grow up or learn something important, even Jesus. We know and sing the Christmas songs about the little town of Bethlehem, because we've heard the story about Jesus being born there. Nazareth is also important because it's where Gabriel told Mary she would give birth to Jesus. It's where we are told Jesus grew up and where He learned something important about humanity.

One of the things Jesus learned was how we might not always be well received, even in our hometown. He'd started His ministry, even performed miracles. I think if we were in Jesus's sandals, we might expect a smidge of a welcome home. In all fairness, they did at first. However, when Jesus read and shared some things they didn't like, they nearly ran him off a cliff. Still, Jesus would forever be associated with this town. If you're the curious type, you might dig a little deeper. The distance between Bethlehem and Nazareth is almost sixty-nine miles. Think hour-long car ride. Back then it may have taken four to five days to walk there. It's four hundred and thirty-two miles from Roanoke, Virginia, to Nashville, Tennessee. That's a six and half–hour drive or one hundred forty-six hours by foot. The journey is a little farther from Clarion, Pennsylvania, where I attended college. We know Jesus is faithful. Still, when I think of all the things He worked out to get me to Nashville, my mind is boggled.

God got me through a consuming freshman year and surrounded me with people who loved me. That group got larger. We had all sorts of socials, large and small group meetings. It fostered growth, a safe place to ask questions, learn, and chances to serve. Being asked to serve as Large Group coordinator meant more than being captain of a football team. In one of the meetings, we performed a DC Talk song. We weren't nearly as good as them, but it took me back to that Weekend of Champions, getting to see the real group perform, and hearing the voice call my name.

A friend had a VHS tape of DC Talk videos. I'd grown up "wanting my MTV" so the idea of music videos was nothing new. The fact that there were now Christian music videos was. I was drawn in, and to see how they'd grown and developed musically was incredible. Approaching senior year with my communications major, I still had to complete an internship. While friends were pursuing spots in the Pittsburgh market, I was pulled to choose something different. One day on the back of the video cover, there it was, a name that would start a southbound path to Music City.

•　　•　　•

Deaton Flanigen Productions was the name of the company that had produced the video. I found their phone number and started calling them every day. The lady who answered phones passed me to their producer, I think it was Kim or Kimberly. She told me they'd never had an intern but would at least present the idea. Eventually, I wore them down and secured an interview. Just before my last fall semester the interview day came—it was August and hot! The day of the interview there was another lesson to be learned. When there are two or more reasonable schools of thought, listen to your gut.

My girlfriend at the time, a marketing major, told me to wear a suit and tie to present a professional image. This went against my instincts. While I'd never been in Nashville or worked in music videos, I'd had some experience. MTV came to our campus to film one of their game shows. Everyone—from host to production— dressed casually. I'd also observed how professional reporters and announcers would frequently wear a nice shirt, maybe a tie or jacket, paired with jeans, sometimes even shorts. However, I listened to her and showed up in a jacket, suit, and tie.

George and Robert were two of the coolest people I'd ever met. Both wearing jeans and a casual shirt, one in cowboy boots, the other in Jordans and a ball cap. I was hot, sweaty, and already nervous. I got the internship and made the appropriate wardrobe change before showing up my first day. Robert later told me they almost said no to the internship because of what I was wearing. Pro tip—go with your gut, people.

It sounds fancy to say you worked in the music video industry. Don't get me wrong, there were surreal moments and unbelievable experiences, but I learned another valuable lesson. We tend to think of famous people as untouchable or unapproachable. It's natural. And sometimes the creative famous people do have a bit of a one-track mind, seem distant, or have a large security detail. My experiences taught me otherwise.

One day we shot a piece for a lady who owns her own amusement park. Yes, that lady. She's at least ten times nicer and more sincere than you think she is. She treated each of us so kindly, like we were part of her family. A few weeks later, we worked with a Better Man who'd be Killin' Time talking about A Bad Goodbye and Walkin' Away. My task for the day was to hold his grapes while he played guitar or hold the guitar while he ate grapes. Again, this guy couldn't have been more genuine or sincere. In between takes, he taught me how to play some chords and let me try them—on his guitar! On another occasion, I caught a bomb. Don't worry, it was a fake bomb, but the fuse was real. It was burning when it was thrown from the stage by a singer with a bunch of rowdy friends. My job was to catch the fake bomb and stay out of the shot. I did, but the hot sparks from the fuse burned my face and sent sparks into my eyes. The first person to me wasn't the director, the first-aid person, or anyone else. It was the singer. I was taken in by how real and genuine each of these people were. A piece of me knew I needed to be here in Nashville, but why? I didn't want to force this, and faith reminded me I'd better pray about it. My gut told me to find a place like the Catholic church in Clarion.

Just down from the office on Music Row was such a church. I had no idea the internship would lead to a job, and I had no clue where the job would lead. But I did know I needed a quiet place to find peace and calm. I started walking over to pray during lunch break. Robert told me it's where the Christian music people go. I did attend their service, thinking maybe the music would be even better than my church back home. The music was good, but I didn't recall seeing anyone famous there. During the week, the doors were open, but rarely did I see a soul in the building.

Occasionally, I'd wave at a secretary or someone who was just walking inside. I was never questioned as to why I was there. Quietly, I would sneak up to the balcony. Just like in Clarion, I would sit, pray, think about life, sing a song, or sometimes even cry. My struggles were still there, even in this new job in a new town. I never could shake it, but I knew coming to a place like this, even alone, brought a genuine calm and peace to the internal struggles I couldn't share.

After weeks of praying alone, out of nowhere there was an Asian lady. She was also upstairs in the balcony but in a different section and in a row higher than mine. She was not there when I arrived. I hadn't heard any noise like someone walking in or talking. She wasn't very close to me, but close enough to know she had to have come up the same stairs I did. I thought I would've heard someone walking up the stairs. A little later I looked, and she was gone. I returned to a quiet prayer. At some point it became tearful.

I was struggling. The time in church provided peace, but I was quietly pleading. God, if you are out there, make it go away. There was a hand on my shoulder and a female Asian voice. Her hand calmed my emotions, and her words were encouraging. I'd calmed down enough to look at her. She was there, a real person, the same lady I'd seen in the other section. She asked how she could pray for me.

I didn't know how to express my angst. I couldn't tell her specifics. I was afraid she'd get up and walk away, or worse, kick me out of the one place providing peace. But she didn't reject me. Her words were specific. She said, "God is going to heal you, and use you and these struggles."

I got a little weirded out. I hadn't ever seen this lady during any previous lunch-break visit or service. I hadn't told her everything. I remember thinking she had to be saying these things just to be nice. She didn't know me or my specifics. I felt myself getting a little angry and thought, How dare she say these things to me! She finished her prayer with me. I echoed her amen, just to be polite. She got up and walked away and I never saw her again.

Confused, I started connecting dots like I had at Clarion. Had my whole life led to this prayer with her? Maybe it was all some cosmic path.

In the weeks to follow, I started writing poems and eventually rap lyrics. Soon there were sheets of paper I called songs. Because of the internship and some folks I'd met at church, I had connected with some people in the music industry. None of them wore wool suits or ties, in case you were wondering. Eventually, I paid a guy to put down some music and create a performance track.

I started to perform for youth groups. Another friend, working for a recording studio, showed interest in taking me on as a potential artist. It all was quickly coming together, but seemed to fade just as fast. I was frustrated and questioned why the doors flew open and just as quickly closed. I thought it was all just another pipe dream delivered by a cruel world and the prayer with the Asian lady. In hindsight it was probably a good thing those pursuits didn't work out. My inner distress—and coping mechanism—was still there, unaddressed. I can see now the doors closed for a reason. But back then I was mad at God.

"Why did my illness lead to the doctor who led me to wrestling and the coaches who pointed me to you?" was most of my prayer, or more accurately, my shouts back at God. *"Why would you save me from killing myself, get me to a Camp, let me hear about DC Talk and hear about you? Why did you call my name that day and give me a glimpse of heaven if I was never going to get rid of this thorn?"* In the silence, I'd wonder if I was even heard. So I'd scream-pray some more. *"I've asked you ten billion times to take this away from me! Were my tears deemed insufficient? Your Bible is full of those healings you had for others and yet nothing for me. Is my heart not sincere? Are my words not worthy of you hearing them? "*

I wondered why I'd been given peace sitting in a church, only to white-knuckle some sense of success, just to fall back so many times. How much could a loving Creator love me, if He just sat there and let this happen again and again? It all seemed sick and twisted to me.

• • •

We don't need to pretend those times were easy. There's a song describing being lost, but then being able to see. Grace was something else I learned in Nashville. Not just grace for others, but for myself too. We may never fully understand our struggles, but occasionally get a glimpse to see He was indeed leading. We are all still a work in progress. It doesn't make us more comfortable or likeable. It doesn't give us a free pass to do whatever we feel like. But we can see a little better now. I recognized all three of those singers were people just like you and me. Each of them had their own demons, their life struggles to overcome, and each did so on their own timetable.

What I've learned is this. Being famous—up on stage, traveling on a tour bus—sounds really cool. But what about us? We are the parents, the teachers, the coaches. We are aunts, uncles, and neighbors. When we focus on not having a famous person's gift, we sell short our gifts, abilities, and calling. Across the board, when those famous people are out on the road, they'd tell you what they miss the most is the exact same stuff we get to do every day. We have the ability, and I daresay the responsibility, to pour into and influence the next generation, the poor, the widowed, the weird neighbor next door, and the man down the street. The one who doesn't want kids on his lawn and doesn't give out candy for Halloween. We can interact and show Jesus's love to the lady at Costco, the homeless person on the corner, the hungry family at the soup kitchen. Each and every one of us has far greater ability to reach out, walk into these spaces, and serve in more ways than any famous singer. Jesus came for all of us, not just the famous ones. He proved this in His hometown of Nazareth.

There would be no cheering crowds, no rock star treatment for this hometown hero. The people of Nazareth had heard of Jesus's preaching and work in other towns. Maybe they thought He'd have an extra-special miracle for His hometown or some insightful teaching. He did, but it wasn't what they wanted to hear. He told them the love of the Father was for everyone, not just the people of Israel. The truth is we don't need a record contract, a tour bus, or millions of followers to do what Jesus tells us to. We should dream big dreams and chase our passions, but let's use our gifts to remind others just how big, deep, and wide God's love is for us. We know how far and how much the love of Jesus has seen us through.

One last thing. Of all the activity we create to better know God, we overlook a simple but important thing—every day, find time for God to love on you. More than prayers, more than praise, more than saying elegant words or singing the perfect song, God wants to love on you. His love is the only one that is pure and unconditional. What might happen if daily we received His love for us, if we listened to the music He's playing for our hearts. Imagine if we allowed that love to fill us every single day. What would our interactions be like? How would we react to someone who expresses an opinion different than ours? Our world needs more peace these days. Letting God love on us is the only way He can fill us with peace. Now more than ever we need it, so we in turn can pour out love and pass along peace to others.

CHAPTER 24

We Don't Understand... Yet

There's a boulder in my backyard. I'm not kidding. It's at least twenty feet in circumference. My friends in Colorado might describe it as just a big rock, but to a guy in southwest Virginia, it's a boulder. Geologists define a boulder as a primarily round rock with curves, smooth edges, and greater than sixteen feet in diameter. That's my boulder. I imagine at one point it was in a wave of frozen ice. Slowly advancing from a far-off place, to end up planted in my backyard. Wouldn't it be interesting to be able to talk with a rock? I think it would be cool, no pun intended. Think how it felt to be carried in a glacier. Imagine being moved by an unseen force. And not to be anticlimactic, I wonder what it's like to have traveled hundreds, if not thousands of miles, to end up basking in sunshine in my backyard. Regardless of how it got there, I suspect the journey was an exciting one.

The Bible mentions moving mountains, but God moves people too. The story of how a former wrestler, football captain, Bob Costas–replacing, music video–making, English teaching, hamburger-flipping, wrestling and football coach from Virginia ends up in Minnesota is equally as surprising.

After nearly a decade of being in business with my parents, it was time for something different. I know a lot of friends thought I was nuts to walk away from a sure thing. But they didn't know what happened behind the scenes. It's both a pleasure and hard to be in a family business. After ten years, and a not-so-clean exit, a search began. I considered everything. There was an embroidery business in Maryland and two different dog kennels, one in Virginia, the other in New Hampshire. I also considered buying a gymnastics gym.

There were three gyms I considered. The first was the closest. I believe the nondisclosure agreement has expired, but the gym in our town was up for sale. I met with the owners, talked about numbers and business, but could never agree on an amount. Next was a gym in Ohio. It was much smaller, and I sensed it wouldn't be a fit. Finally, there was a gym in Minnesota. I'd searched the "business for sale" websites. But once, I googled gyms for sale. On the fifth page a listing intrigued me. I think it was the broken English describing the business that first caught my attention. There was an exchange of emails, also in broken English. I figured this was either a legit business for sale, an elaborate scheme by a foreign country, or possibly a teenager attempting to phish information from me.

Fortunately, it was a very kind Serbian couple selling their business. This explained the broken English. She was a powerful gymnast, and he was a world-class Shotokan karate expert; both had competed internationally. Admittedly, I was a little intimidated. Outside of watching the practice of a younger sister, my only gymnastics experience was back when I was in kindergarten and a two-week gymnastics lesson in a high school PE class. Perhaps it was a refined version of naive confidence, but the years of previous experience whispered to me. I'd moved to Nashville and jumped into an industry with no real experience. I'd spent years selling copiers and office furniture, not to mention my time in the family business. And most significant was the experience of having been a teacher.

I so admired the teachers and coaches I had growing up. My self-confidence was the cumulative impact of their lesson plans. It didn't matter if it was math problems or how to write a term paper. It wasn't about wrestling an opponent, and it had nothing to do with making a tackle. The truth they instilled with their countless hours of lesson or practice plans was now a calm sense of you can do this. I may not have had the personal competitive experience, but I had worked with kids. While I'd only sold physical objects like fax machines, office chairs, and hamburgers, I knew life lessons learned from being active in sports. It had been a huge part of my life. At one point those teammates and coaches had literally saved my life. Taking a leap of faith and running your own business is life-changing, both good and bad. I mustered up the courage, purchased the business, and started a grand new adventure.

I didn't have any illusions of coaching my kids to the Olympics. Not because I didn't think they could make it, but because I'd just figured there was more to sports. In fact, the idea of investing in the passion and desire of kids played a big factor in convincing myself I could make it all work. I also needed a job and while the prospect of moving halfway across the country was daunting, I did it. Now I just had to figure out a sport I didn't know, how to run my own business, and how to fit in where people didn't say y'all. My training in broadcasting allowed me to readopt a Midwestern accent pretty quickly.

I started with cleaning and taught preschool classes. Two weeks in, I ran my first payroll. Everyone got paid and no checks bounced. I'd met with team-parents and children, answered their questions and things were going well. For the first year and a half, I spent more time at the gym than I did in my rented apartment. But it ended up being for the best. It allowed me to go all in. I poured myself into this business, the same way I had attacked athletics and everything else in life. I mastered a morning cleaning schedule, did administrative tasks during the day, and assisted classes during the evening. It was exhausting. They say there's nothing like owning your own business and they're right. I'd never worked so hard in my life.

When the pre-team coach left, I jumped in. Doing so helped make connections between the curriculum I'd been teaching in the preschool class. I could see how it advanced. Despite not having competed in gymnastics, there seemed to be an advantage to coaching a sport I hadn't done. When I coached football and wrestling, I knew the ins and outs. I knew pursuit angles, and which side my head should be on when blocking or tackling. I knew what it felt like to get small, create space, and get a reversal. I knew what it meant to explode out from the bottom position. I knew all of this from having done it. But it's hard to teach the "feel" of a sport, and I struggled communicating this to the young men I coached.

Conversely, not knowing the feel and timing of gymnastics made me a better coach for novice kids. And when they said, "I can't do it!" I called them on it. Partly because I was sometimes telling myself the same thing about coaching this new sport (and also, for the first time, coaching young ladies). But the same three-letter word I kept telling myself is the same word I made them learn. I'd stop whatever drill we were working on and gather them all together. Sometimes I put the girl who'd said, "I can't" on the spot by repeating it to the group. I told them I don't like the word can't. Now I know you are already flashing back to my track experiment. And maybe it's because of that experience, I was able to relate to their frustrations. I told them, "Can't means you are quitting or giving up," and I'd say they didn't seem like quitters or someone who gives up to me. I reminded them the things we were learning to do were hard. I'd point to their previous success of mastering new things.

Keep in mind, the girls I coached were between four and six years old. I always got a smile by asking, "Hey, when you were born, did you come out of your Mommy's tummy being able to walk and talk? Did you already know how to pick out your own clothes, eat and drink, or use the bathroom?" You could tell right away who had younger siblings. They'd help make my point by sharing stories of younger siblings crawling, standing up or using a bottle. And of course, there were extra giggles when they mentioned dirty, stinky diapers. Ultimately, we found a middle ground and I taught them my favorite three-letter word. They could say "I can't do it" but only if they added the word yet! It took them awhile, but they started to encourage each other. Even the newer girls knew what to add when they slipped up and saw my expectant big eyes. Together we all learned to cut ourselves a little slack. They taught themselves and taught each other to remember the yet. They even took care of helping me to teach the new girls who came to our ever-growing group. This included a young lady who eventually taught me more than I could've ever taught her. Let's call her Addy.

● ● ●

When Addy came to the group, she was already eight. A little older, but right away her ability to listen and make changes had potential written all over it. She never spoke a lot of words, but always had a big smile. It took a couple months to get her to say more than just her name. I circled back with her mom and dad, just to see if there was anything I was missing or should know about their daughter. They both said they weren't aware of anything, but lately she was just being quiet. They both assured me she was enjoying her gymnastics time and did, in fact, talk about all the fun and new things she was learning. I thought nothing of it and figured it would just take time. Time was well spent; Addy quickly became a leader and her skills allowed her to be a demonstrator for the group. It surprised no one when she was promoted to team and qualified for the state championships her first year.

My favorite event to coach was vault and this just happened to be one of Addy's best events. At the state meet, vault was our third event. I'd been keeping an eye on vault scores and the highest I'd seen was 9.5. Addy had bested the score several times during the year. I started to think that if anyone was worthy of the state title, it would be this quiet, always smiling, hard-working athlete. We made it to vault and eventually it was her turn.

The reason I like vault so much is because it requires the athlete to run as fast as their legs can carry them. At the last second, they hurdle their feet in front, punching the springboard with their legs in a straight, tight shape. By remaining tight, the board does the work of transferring the energy from the run. Then they get to fly. Granted, even the Olympic gymnasts only fly for a second, maybe two. But even at this level Addy understood the importance of staying "tight in flight." She scored a 9.85. I was so happy for her—and the smile on her face was bigger than ever. Unfortunately, the next rotation of vaulters had two 9.9's and a 9.95. So I made the decision to break the rules.

In my gym we had a rule: if you finished in the top three at state, you earned a banner with your name, and all the specifics about your state score. Addy's 9.85 put her in fourth that year. However, the thing about making rules is you can change them. You better believe I changed the rule to the top five at state. If anyone should have their name on the wall, it was Ms. Addy.

The day the banner went up, Addy was all smiles. Then came the day. Mom and Dad wanted to speak with me after practice. They shared their decision to move closer to the cities. It meant Addy would no longer train with us. We left on great terms and Addy continued competing, just for a different gym. Occasionally at meets, we'd see her or her parents. It was both sad and happy.

Addy's banner remained at our gym. And I can't tell you how many times I pointed it out to a struggling gymnast. I'd tell them about the quiet girl who didn't say a lot of words, but kept smiling, kept fighting for skills. Even though she was gone, her story and how she carried herself taught so many other girls how to persist in the hard times.

●　　●　.　●

It took a few years until I learned just how hard things were for her.

Years later, I'd sold the gym. The new owner mentioned he wasn't going to keep the banners. Fortunately, the young lady he'd selected to manage this location suggested taking the banners down and offering them to the girls who'd earned them. This eventually led to seeing Addy one more time. She and her mom came to the gym. We talked about how much had changed, both in the gym and the young lady I once coached. Addy was about to enter her senior year of high school and was still smiling. It got even bigger when she saw the banner she'd earned years earlier. We parted ways and I asked her mom to keep me up to date on all the events of Addy's senior year. She did, and as I moved away from Minnesota, the social media updates were much appreciated. Addy's mom pored through pictures for a graduation party, and I received a message revealing just how big our God is.

As the owner of a small gym, I'd worn many hats, and sometimes a wig. We hosted a rock star–themed meet and one of my jobs was announcing awards. I did this dressed as Robbie the Rock Star, complete with pants way too tight, a tie-dyed shirt, and a spiked wig that for one day gave me more hair than the girls I coached. Addy's mom had sent a picture of a much younger Addy, next to me in that getup, both posing with a big smile. I thanked her for sharing, commented on good times, and what a pleasure it was to coach her daughter. I wasn't prepared for her response: "You have no idea how much you and your gym changed Addy's life. Her learning disabilities and struggles to communicate were so profound it led her to feeling suicidal in the third grade. We didn't know or understand anything then. But gymnastics gave her a confidence we only saw glimpses of. I can't ever express our gratitude for what you did."

I don't readily admit to big ugly cries, but it was all I could do. It was hard to read about pain and struggle faced by the quiet, hard-working, but always smiling young lady I'd coached years ago. Yet it filled my heart that a parent first trusted me with their child, and then shared her story. Dots connected. I realized I was only there to coach her—because a coach had been there for me.

In an instant, God can reveal how big He is. It wasn't dumb luck that a football player and wrestler from Virginia who'd also faced suicide would "just happen" to buy a gym in Minnesota. A gym where this girl's parents would "just happen" to enroll their eight-year-old. That their child "just happened" to be struggling with hard thoughts and "just happened" to end up in my group. And even though I had quit track and it took me years to figure things out, I, her coach, was teaching a message about steady persistence and not ever giving up.

Don't believe in coincidence. Believe the same forces that moved a boulder to my backyard had intervened. We can believe that no matter how dire our circumstances, God will do it again. God chooses to interweave the lives of people. He doesn't always choose the most talented or those with the right experience. He's not bound by a difference in gender, age, or geographic location. God loves you and even though it feels like you can't make it, know this. When it seems everything is against you, when you feel like quitting, keep going. God will see it through. Maybe what you long for happens or maybe another boulder gets moved halfway across the country. You will make it; it just hasn't happened … yet.

CHAPTER 25

When Most Things Head South

There were waves of snowfall in the parking lot. The wind formed them as snow blew everywhere. Depending on where I stepped, the snow was ankle high or thigh deep. If you've spent any amount of time living in the Midwest, you know what I'm talking about. My first winter in Minnesota was 2010 and it just happened to be the fourth snowiest since the state started tracking weather in 1819. That's only because an army fort was built.

Fort Snelling is a former military fort and currently on the list of National Historic Landmarks. It was built on land overlooking the spot where the Minnesota and Mississippi Rivers combine on their southward journey out of the state. Fort Snelling wasn't always its name. As it was being built, the site was known as Fort Saint Anthony, which is ironic. Anthony is reportedly the saint in charge of all things lost. And after ten years of growing the business, expanding not once but twice, I'd lost nearly everything important to me. I think just like a fort can have two different names, we humans have two different forces pushing and pulling us in every decision.

Back when I'd moved out here it was for a chance to own my own business, provide resources, and have a say over when I worked.

• • •

I was doing things differently than the previous owners. It was a good gym, but I always wanted it to be better. Within an hour's drive of our place, were two of the top five Junior Olympic gymnastics gyms in the entire country. They both produced countless college scholarships and multiple US national team members. I didn't imagine our little gym would overtake them; I just knew we could be better.

But people resist change. I could handle push-back from parents, but I've heard others say it's especially hard when it's your child on the receiving end from other kids who don't like the changes. I imagine it's hard when supposed teammates blame you for changes they don't like. I don't think there is a parent on the planet who wants their child to be picked on, but the only outcomes I saw were making my small business dream more of a nightmare. I'd like to say I handled it well, but I really didn't. On a good day, it felt like I was spinning my wheels between the deep snowbanks, struggling to manage all the relationships and responsibilities. And those were the good days. The bad days felt like being shackled and trapped at Fort Snelling. For ten years the dance continued. There were different moves and challenges that all presented themselves. Some I handled better than others. There were highs of state championships and individual honors. And lows of increasing strains and rocky relationships.

• • •

I hoped 2020 was going to be a great year. Despite my private struggles, September would officially mark a decade of owning the kids' activity center. It had grown from being a small gym to mid-size. We had more gymnastics teams and classes, and the quality was better than ever. We'd reinvested heavily in our facilities. The preschool programs I started with years ago were growing and now took over the former dance studio. That happened with the second expansion, when dance moved from a single studio, to three. And the ninja program that started with four kids in a single class was now nearly one hundred kids in a dozen classes. I was exhausted and joyful. Then March came, but the month known for golden rainbows, green clovers and good luck would become marked by something altogether different.

Some people think teachers only work nine months out of the year and enjoy summers off. In a similar way, some people thought I only worked when practice or classes were happening. When most of us think of business owners we think of corporate offices, CEOs, and pension plans that could make eyes pop. Small business owners are a different breed. Most small business owners don't have the normal nine-to-five. These owners typically wear many hats. Most, by choice or need, spend a regular day working in the business. This might be interacting with clients or helping with the many tasks to care for and deliver product or services to the customers. Before or after this day, there is often an entirely different workday, working on the business. These are the unseen, untracked hours, tucked away in an office doing the not-so-glamorous work. Crunching numbers, tracking ins and outs, paying bills and employees—these are just a few of the administrative tasks. When we aren't doing either of those we are trying to sleep or lying in bed thinking of our other two jobs.

It took me a while, but I slowly realized owning my business was costing me the very reasons I bought the business. To the public, we were a thriving, well respected small business. We were known and active in the community. Our parents were vocally supportive. I always felt we were understaffed, but what we lacked in quantity, we had in quality. No staff is perfect, but ours was genuine, hard-working, dedicated, caring folks who parents and children could trust.

Privately, there were differences in opinion and tensions would occasionally surface amongst staff. This wasn't any different than any workplace I'd ever experienced. Outside of work, things were different too. I began to question why I was doing this and wondered if all the effort was worth it.

There are several reasons people list for leaving a job. Salary, work-life balance, moving, other opportunities, lack of mobility, and need for a change are just a few. The list of reasons why I had started to think about selling my business wasn't much different.

It's easy to think business owners have a great salary and money somehow makes it all worth it. I thought that way too. But when I considered ten years of six- or seven-day weeks, with ten to fifteen hours a day, the hourly rate was painful. There was no work-life balance. I was either worrying about the kids I coached, trying to help the stressors of my coaches, or cleaning up messes at the gym, or at home. I was tired just from physically moving that much in a day and the constant day-to-day struggles of running a business. Enter COVID-19.

We joined the rest of the world by shutting down. Our state mandated a quarantine for the rest of March and all of April and May. While this provided a break from long work weeks, it also meant new problems. Things like, how does the business pay rent? How do I pay employees? How do I justify charging families when children can't come? All of these and others became more reasons to consider selling the business.

I listed it for sale in late November of 2020. I didn't know what would happen in the year to come but I knew I could trust God to help sort it all out. The week after I listed it for sale, our state shut down businesses again, in an attempt to squash the spread over the holidays. We couldn't reopen until January of '21. The mass shooting so close to our gym happened in February. It prompted the conversation with my little ninja, which prompted writing this book. I had no idea what I was doing. It was all surreal, but too real. I read it all as arrows pointing to an exit. But from what to what? I realize not everyone owns or sells a business, but I bet most understand or experienced hard things like a hard medical diagnosis, strained relationships, concerns about children, and not really knowing what is coming next.

● ● ●

It's during these times, when things seem most uncertain, when we don't see what God is working out, that faith can seem to fail us. It doesn't really. God is always at work sorting things out and getting us from point A to point B. But just like those rivers come together by Fort Snelling, things beyond my control were happening and it all headed south.

Can you trust me this much? Jesus might have pointed to this question but never asked it while He was here. But the Holy Spirit most certainly calls us to experience a deeper relationship by whispering this question in every situation, both the good times and bad. It's precisely when chaos and uncertainty surround us that our faith is defined.

The calendar rolled over to a new year and the first offer to buy the business came in. Ironically, from the guy who owned one of the top two gyms. I said no. Driven by multiple inputs, I still meandered like a river between its banks. I was trying to find what was the right thing to do. I didn't know where God was leading, but both selling and continuing to run the business seemed like a death sentence for the people I cared about most. Part of me knew I had to stick it out, at least until June. The guy came back with other offers in March and April; I said no again. In June, graduation season had come and gone. In July, came an offer worth considering.

It wasn't an amount to retire on, but it would allow a smoother transition out of Minnesota, perhaps back to Virginia. There had been multiple reasons perfectly aligning to form an arrow, of sorts, pointing back home. One of them was that I'd been contemplating ways to reconcile the divide between me and my parents. Being in the same state was no guarantee but seemed like a move in the right direction.

I'd end up accepting the offer late in the summer, but as in any undertaking of this nature, there were documents to sign and legalese to interpret. It ended our business and, sadly, answered other questions as well. The plan was for me to stay at the gym for a while to help smooth the transition for staff and kids. There would be one final Thanksgiving in Minnesota.

During this time, I was caught between two rivers. What would I do for a living? Where was I going to move? I was exhausted in every possible way, physically, mentally, emotionally, and even spiritually. I felt strongly the new owner could take the business places I hadn't been able to. I knew it was time to sell but still didn't know what was next. I left every option on the table, even a return to working for my parents. I attempted to set up interviews in Virginia, but no one wanted to talk with me until I was back in the state. The jobs I sought weren't glamorous but would provide a living wage. Combined with the terms of the sale, I saw it all as a path back to Virginia and hopefully a fresh start.

It's hard when only parts of a plan are known. My church offered quiet times of prayer and for about five years, my time was Friday night from ten to eleven. Every week I'd ask and pray, God, what's next now? There were no burning bushes, and no voice boomed down from parted clouds or up from parted waters. But through it all was a quiet, steady, whispered question. Can you trust me this much?

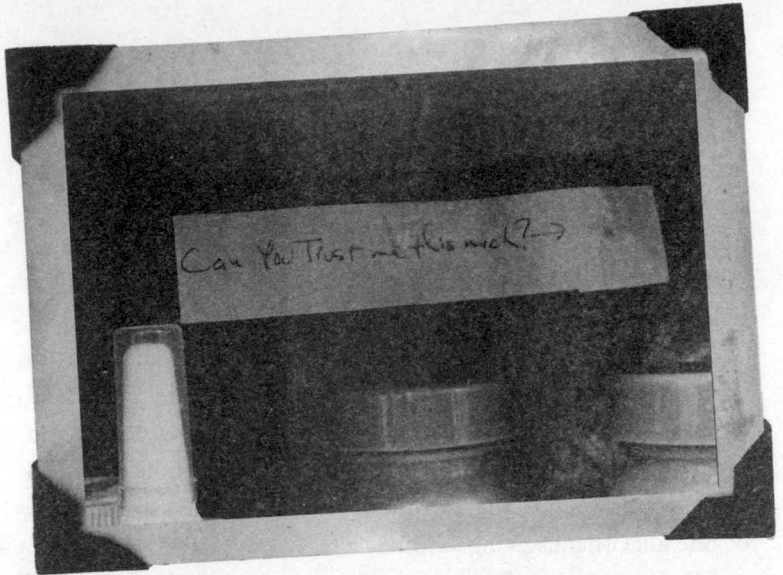

CHAPTER 26

The Question

C an you trust me this much? It's a question Jesus never asked while He was here. We could argue He hinted at the idea as He talked about the smallest of seeds. Maybe the disciples saw something in His expression or heard trustworthiness in His voice. We think how good those first believers had it. But I think sometimes we neglect the gift Jesus left us.

Most of our prayers start, "Dear heavenly Father" or "Lord, Jesus" ("Sweet baby Jesus" if your name is Ricky Bobby) and there is nothing wrong with those prayers. Kidding aside, Jesus promised we wouldn't be left alone. He left us an advocate. In His absence, He promised the third part of the posse would be with us until He returns. Too often we miss out on a living faith with a living spirit. We wouldn't settle for two-thirds of our paycheck. We wouldn't settle for watching two-thirds of the summer blockbuster we've been waiting to see. So why would we settle for two-thirds of a relationship with God? Here's the good news—we don't have to. God's Spirit is readily accessible 24/7, and He's given us the not-so-secret passwords. Ask, seek, and knock.

A gym parent shared a story telling me they'd never forget the year their child asked Santa for a balance beam. They, I mean Santa, somehow got it down the chimney. The excitement was priceless. They'd watch hours of practicing skills (instead of doing homework). That was until they negotiated verbal spelling tests on the beam. Every correct word earned a cartwheel attempt. That beam was loved and used daily for years. It let those parents know they—as parents and Santa—had given a good gift. Their story reminds me of just how much more God wants to give us the gifts of His Spirit. While asking for help is a first step, we also must listen. The call of the Spirit won't shout above the noise of our daily lives. Just like God and Jesus, this Spirit is inviting us, calling us, to a deeper faith in every situation—the good, the bad, and the ugly.

Each day the question is whispered to our souls. Can you trust me this much? Our lives are filled with good and wonderful times. And we've lived long enough to know there will also be troublesome, faith-shaking times. Regardless of how we grew up or what we're experiencing now, the question remains a steady call, a choice we make every moment of every day. We all want the happy ending, but even when it seems like God, Jesus, and the Spirit are silent, there is wisdom to be gained. Active listening means making time to be still, wherever we are. We can do this at work or home, by a closed window or an open door.

I've never parachuted, but I've heard both fear and excitement are strongest standing by the open door above the drop zone. The Bible mentions putting away the things of a child, our old ways of thinking. This applies to all aspects of our lives. Our lives will have change. Change is constant and can be scary. Peace is most often found in our persistent seeking and knocking. A friend of mine even makes the case for this concept applying to our jobs. He says just because you are good at a certain job, doesn't mean it's still a good job for the person you are becoming. Our Father, His Son, and the Spirit are constantly at work moving each of us along the journey of who they are making us to be. The same tension felt by a parachute jumper was my life for the last three and a half years in Minnesota, so I jumped and sold the business.

People thought I had, again, lost my mind, that I hadn't thought it through or was only thinking of myself. I was relatively young and had invested a decade building a respectable business. Many asked, why leave now? Truth be told, part of me wondered the same thing. In many ways the families at the gym were way more than customers or clients, they were like family. But something had been changing inside me. The slow steady growth of the business mimicked the ascent of a plane. We'd made it through the turbulence of starting something new, my learning all aspects of the business, and the sport of gymnastics. We'd climbed above most of our staffing and programming challenges. We pulled it out from the nosedive of state-mandated closures and the resulting staff departures. We made it past important personal and business milestones. I had given my all and grown it as big as I could ... I was exhausted and had nothing left.

Prayer is one way to ask, seek, and knock. I'd spent years praying. My prayers were always for the necessary things to keep the business strong. Things like staff, clients, patience, wisdom, resources—they all appeared at just the right time. When those stopped showing up, it had my full attention. This didn't stop my prayers, it just added something. We all experience changes in life, and over the years, God had helped me tune in to His Spirit. It's not easy and I'm not claiming to own the red blinking, bat phone, directly connected to heaven. But God knows our inclination to cling to what we know. Rather than giving us the detailed big picture plan, the Spirit will give us the gentle suggestions and soft nudges we need to take the first step. And when we miss or ignore the gentle ones, more jarring methods of attention-getting can be implored. Those nudges (be they gentle or jarring) come from prayers open, honest, and bold enough to ask, God, if you need me to do something different, lead me there. Here I am Lord, use me.

We know the incredible stories of parents, pastors, coaches, or teachers who enjoyed a single career. They gave thirty or forty years; they got the retirement party and the gold watch. In some ways, I envy a life like that. More recently, the world and its economic state are constantly changing, and so are we. Saying we believe in the Father, Son, and Spirit is one thing. Living it is another. For some of us, a single marriage, a single career doesn't happen. And I think sometimes our choices don't always mesh with who God is calling us to be. I'm not suggesting God is pro-divorce or approves of hopping from job to job. I am saying, life is full of questions, decisions, and change. Sometimes, we are going to flat out mess it up. God isn't panicked when we zig instead of zag. In an ever-changing world, His vision of who He is guiding us to be is unwavering. He reaches for another reserve parachute and moves us toward who and what we need to be. I knew selling was the right thing to do. I believed with all my heart it was a win for everyone and everything. The future growth of the business, coaching for the kids, and the remnants of family.

What do we do when the main chute doesn't open, when our best-laid plans fall apart? We can panic and second-guess our choices. Or trust God to reach deeper into His abundant reserve. God doesn't lead us to a desert or fly us over a drop zone just to abandon us. He's got plans for each of us and endless reserves of mercy and grace. We all want—but don't need to know—all the answers. Our minds aren't made to comprehend all possibilities. And sure, it would be great if life had no troubles. Life is scariest above the drop zone. But it's easier when we ask, seek, and knock. It helps us to learn to trust God to be God. He, in turn, will help us focus on our three responsibilities.

The first can be tough. We have to trust our advocate. We know life experiences can hinder our ability to trust others and even God. Our Father is bigger than any misstep we could ever make. He knows our choices, both good and bad. He knew how our humanity would play out. He provided all the reserves we would ever need when He sent His Son. Our second job is to listen - listen to the Spirit. Don't get me wrong: it's not easy to hear the small voice whispering while humanity is screaming in our ear. It's like listening to the commands of a jump instructor while standing at the open door high above the drop zone. And finally, we need to jump!

When I jumped, I wasn't 100 percent clear on what would happen next, and I'm still not. I did know that just like Minnesota winters slowly give way to spring, the season there had ended. The house in Minnesota sold after that last Thanksgiving. People who were more than friends parted ways. It would be easy to wonder why the chute didn't open on the fairy tale ending. It's possible to second-guess the decisions we make. I could've stayed at the gym, crossed my fingers, and hoped for the best.

But to do so would've meant not jumping. We can choose to not jump. We can choose to not put on a chute, or even not get on the plane. But this doesn't stop the work of the Spirit. By giving us freedom to choose, God made us human. He knew inevitably we'd use that same ability and choose to hurt each other. He knew this would make it hard for us to trust Him. Life is a series of unpacking hurts and relearning trust. But in relearning to trust God, He allows us to mine nuggets of hope and courage from the empty shafts where we spent years digging and working hard. And more often we find pearls of new purpose along the shore, previously locked up in shells of shattered dreams.

We can learn to cut others some slack. People like spouses both present and past, our parents and grandparents, our teachers, coaches, and former class or teammates. All the people who've impacted our lives. They did the very best they could. They had challenges. They knew hurts too; they had pains we didn't ever see.

We can learn to persevere. Whether it's playing sports, being an employee or employer, a loving spouse, being a parent, or just figuring out how to be God's child. Our job isn't to have it all figured out by a certain age; we just have to take the next step.

We can learn that troubles and hard times don't go away just because we love Jesus. And just like Paul's thorn, some of our trials, addictions, and the things we like least about ourselves are going to remain hanging in our flesh. Don't be disgusted by them; instead, trust they serve a higher purpose and don't be surprised when that very painful experience is used to help someone else.

We can learn to be loved on. We tend to fill our lives with activity and our prayer lists with needs. If there is one thing God most wants to do for us, it's love on us. Let's learn to let God love on us. That's not putting ourselves before others and not making ourselves more important than God. But if we are indeed His hands and feet, if we are His vessels here on earth, being loved on is essential. An empty vessel can't hold water, mercy, grace, or love. And don't worry if you are feeling broken from events of the past— God loves using our brokenness to pour out more of His love.

We can learn to learn. That means being open to change. No matter how strong our conviction "feels" in the moment. His truth is in His word. We can look for the burning bush and listen for the voice from on high, but we can't ignore the quiet steady tug of His heart. Jesus spent His life seeking out the people groups everyone else wanted to dismiss, send away, or brush off to the side. If we really want to be more like Jesus, we must do the same. Be open to receiving another piece of the puzzle that might completely change our perspective. Let's keep seeking the kaleidoscope of God's heart for humanity. God doesn't change, but He doesn't ever stop changing our hearts to be more like His.

Imagine that twenty years ago Gabriel himself had come to me and said, *"Hey, I, uh, need you to leave your teaching and coaching job and go spend a decade working for your parents. That will end a little bumpy. Oh, and after that, I need you to move halfway across the country. You are going to take over a kid's activity center, you're going to learn and coach a sport you know nothing about. Because that time you wanted to kill yourself, yeah we're going to use that to help one of those kids, and you won't know it happened until years later. Oh, and speaking of years later, eventually there will be a mass shooting nearby that will prompt a conversation with a five-year-old ninja. I know you don't know what a ninja is yet, but trust me, it's going to be big! That conversation will turn you around. You are going to write it all down, as in write a book. In the process you will get a glimpse of how God moved. Speaking of moving, you'll eventually move back to Virginia, lose some relationships, and things will be strained. I know this is a lot but don't worry, you'll make it."*

I assure you I would've responded to this with a hard pass. But because the Father, the Son, and Spirit know our human limits, they work differently, giving us just enough to take the next step.

If I had a DeLorean and could go back in time, I think I know how I could've better answered the question of the five-year-old ninja. It's the same answer I've learned to give five-year-old me and all previous versions of me. It's the same way a loving parent consoles their child when something goes bump in the night. It's the same answer our heavenly Father gives us when things go bump in our lives. It's the same in-depth answer the Spirit gives us when our despair and angst hit the fan: What happened is horrible. I know how scary it was for you. It was wrong. But I am using all of it to make things better, to make it right.

He exchanges our hurts with the smallest of seeds and asks, Can you trust me this much? Place this seed in the gaping wound of your heart, bury it in the hole of your hurt. Trust it is not forgotten but planted. Trust that your tears are joined by mine, my Son's, and all those who've likewise suffered. Together our tears will water the seed. What your eyes now see as dirt and the mess of all your mistakes are the soil I use to nourish and protect the seed. It will grow into the new thing I am doing in you. And even though you can't always see me or what I am doing—trust. Trust that I see the end version. Trust. I am at work, and I am using this to get you there.

We know it can be frustrating at best, heartbreaking at worst, when any chapter of life comes to its end. The emotional noise clatters and hinders our ability to hear and trust anyone, let alone an unseen spirit. It would be a happily-ever-after if we all experienced the same calling, at the same time, to the same things. But God doesn't work like this. We do know that God works all things out for the good of those who love Him, and still, He gives us choice.

We are His created creatures. In our frail human nature, we prefer chasing the creature comforts and doing our best to avoid the wisdom learned through pain, hurts, and giving our honest answer to the Spirit's question of trust. Just as we grow in human form, God planted His seed in each of us and calls our spirit to grow. The very things we seek to avoid are what He needs us to go through, feel, and experience. It's a process. Each of us on our own pace, learning and growing in grace and the courage to answer, "Yes, your will, not mine, be done."

Despite the hurts we know will come, despite our fears and self-doubt, we can take the next step and jump! We can trust God to be God, the Creator who loves us. We can close our eyes, open our hearts, and know the love as we gaze into the eyes of Jesus. And to the Spirit who swirls in and amongst us, nudging (or jarring) us, and revealing a thumb ever so close to an index finger. May we be bold enough to answer a simple yes each time we are asked, Can you trust me this much?

Acknowledgments

To my family … thank you for raising me and for the experiences in this book. You formed me.

To my teachers and coaches … you continued the work my family started, and I thank you.

To everyone from Buffalo, Minnesota, Gym Nation, and The Dance Academy… I love you. I hope I taught and helped you as much as you did for me. These experiences formed me and indirectly you.

Finally, **to Jamie, Kim, Bob, Brandon, Tim and the tribe of people I met at The Oaks** a few months after the shooting, this book doesn't exist without you.

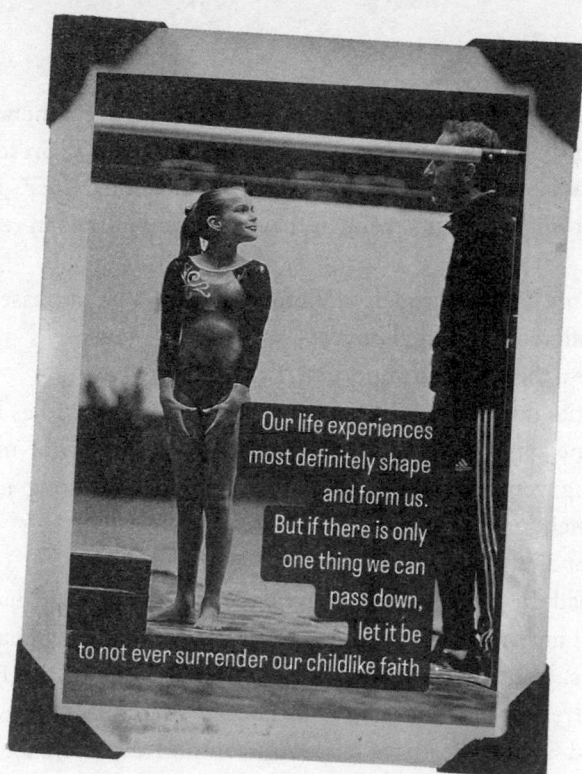

Our life experiences most definitely shape and form us. But if there is only one thing we can pass down, let it be to not ever surrender our childlike faith

Appendix

First, thank you for coming alongside me on this journey. The goal was to illustrate that we are not alone. I recognize our life experiences may be similar and others vastly different. However, if aspects of my story prompted you to discover or revisit parts of yours, then we've had success. I also know that for some there are parts of our journey that are hard to talk about. I did a Google search, you can do one, too, but here's a partial list of what I found:

• Spend your time doing something you enjoy. Yes, you can also cry about your loss, grief, and painful experiences.

• Move your body. Indoors, outdoors? You pick.

• Take control of your anxiety or depression. See a therapist. You might also consider seeing a doctor who'd prescribe antidepressants or other mental health medications. There have been vast improvements made in these pharmaceuticals in recent years.

• Serve others through volunteering. You'd be surprised at what a difference this might make.

• See a therapist. So important, I've said it twice.

• Write down your emotions in a journal. Many studies have been done on this; it's a powerful tool for clearing your mind, organizing your thoughts, and calming yourself, among many other benefits.

What did I do?

• Read the Bible. Here, I didn't cite scripture in each chapter because I am one of those who is terrible at memorizing chapter and verse. Jesus told memorable stories and if one of the Bible stories I referenced throughout the book, speaks to you, we've organized all the references here. You can find the reference and dig in a little deeper.

• Next for me was getting active in specific activities I was interested in. I think the smart people call this self-care. I just call it having a hobby. Equally effective is seeking the opportunities to serve others. But don't forget what my Dad says: "There's a tension" between those two. Exclusive use of one inherently denies the other.

• Music - If you've ever had a favorite song, you know the power of music. If books were like movies, they'd have a soundtrack. There are any number of musical styles and artists who'd make my soundtrack. Several are listed in the pages of this book and new ones emerge every day. If this book ever gets made into a movie, the soundtrack will be epic! But my list of favorites is not nearly as important as yours. Who would be on your list? Try to write at least enough to fill the soundtrack for your life story. Re-listen to those songs and reconnect with the message that first got your attention.

• Nature – I spent nearly two decades working inside of first my parents' restaurant and then the gym. My advice to me, to you, would be to get outside. It doesn't matter if you like hiking in mountains or strolling along lake shores. Whether you like hot sunny beaches or skiing down cold snowy slopes. Let's not argue over which is better, both sunrises and sunsets are awesome! Nature is God's canvas, and He makes some crazy good masterpieces that take your breath away and at the same time restore your soul.

• For me, writing things down is incredibly helpful. It's what started the journey of writing this book. I highly recommend it! Get all of it out—the good, the bad, the painful, the tears and screams. God says it's all valid.

• Finally, see a therapist. Have I mentioned this already? Sometimes in Christian circles we minimize the resource of mental health experts. Don't do that. Pastors and friends can be a great resource and point you in the right direction, but even on their best day, they are still a friend or a pastor. Their primary task is not your mental health. Seeking a professional is not that different than those conversations we've held with a good coach, mentor, or that favorite teacher of yours. The big difference being that as our coaches and teachers were trained, and have specific expertise and knowledge in their field, a mental health professional is all about helping you be a better you.

References & Footnotes

An Introduction
- Isaiah 43:18–19 (things He is making anew)
- 2 Corinthians 12:9 (my grace is sufficient for you)
- 2 Corinthians 12:9–10 (when I am weak, then I am strong)
- Ecclesiastes 4:12 (cord of three strands)

Chapter 1: "All Aboard"
- 1 Corinthians 13:13 (the greatest of these is love)
- Psalm 46:10 (Be still and know I am God)
- Matthew 4:19 (Follow me)

Chapter 2: She's a Mother
- Matthew 18:3 (He said to inherit heaven we had to be more like the children)
- 1 Chronicles 16:11 (Look to the LORD and his strength; seek his face ` always)
- 1 Chronicles 22:19 (Now devote your heart and soul to seeking the LORD your God)
- Acts 17:27 (God did this so that they would seek him … though he is not far from any one of us)
- Jeremiah 29:13 (You will seek me and find me when you seek me with all your heart)
- Matthew 6:33 (But seek first his kingdom and … all these things will be given to you as well)
- Proverbs 8:17 (I love those who love me, and those who seek me find me)
- Psalm 9:10 (For you LORD, have never forsaken those who seek you)
- Luke 11:9–10 (Ask and it will be given to you; seek and you will find; knock …)

Chapter 3 A Smaller World
- Lu:ke 15:1–7 (the shepherd who leaves the ninety-nine to search for one)

Chapter 4: Closer to the Truth
- Luke 19:1–10 (Zacchaeus)
- 1 John 3:18 (Dear children, let us not love with words or speech but with actions and in truth.)
- 1 Chronicles 28:9 and 2 Chronicles 15:2 (if we seek God, we can find Him)
- Psalm 46:10 (be still and listen, or actually Be still and know that I am God)

Chapter 5: Little League Life Lessons
- John 2:1–11 (water into wine, saving best to last)
- Matthew 15:32–39 (feeding the four thousand)
- Mark 8:10–18 (the yeast of the Pharisees and Herod)

Chapter 6: How Can I get There from Here?
- Matthew 18:23–35 (the unforgiving servant)

- Luke 13:10–13 (crippled woman who was suddenly able to stand because Jesus forgave her)
- Luke 15:4–7 (the lost sheep)
- Luke 15:11–32 (the prodigal son)
- Luke 23:34 (Father, forgive them for they know not)
- John 20:19, 21, 26 (rather than disown Peter for denying Him, He offered forgiveness and peace three times)
- Mark 2:5 (He told the paralytic, "Child, your sins are forgiven")
- Luke 7:48 (a sinful woman bathed his feet with her tears and wiped them with her hair)
- John 8:11 (whoever is without sin can cast the first stone)
- Luke 23:43 ("Today you will be with me in paradise")

Chapter 7: Truth and Peace
- Matthew 7:7 (ask and it will be given, seek and you will find, knock)
- John 14:6 (I am the way the truth and the life)
- Matthew 21:12–17 (the cleansing of the temple when Jesus flipped over tables)
- Matthew 5:9 (blessed are the peacemakers)

Chapter 8: Being Broken
- Matthew 22:38–39 (the first of these is love; and the second ...)
- [1]Daniel H. Robinson, Alexander H. Toledo, "Historical development of modern anesthesia," National Library of Medicine, National Center for Biotechnology Information, June 2012, https://pubmed.ncbi.nlm.nih.gov/22583009/ (accessed November 2022)

Chapter 9: Games We Play
- John 8:11 (let those among you who is without sin cast the first stone)
- John 14:12 (those who have faith in me will do what I've done and even greater)
- John 8:11 (Neither do I condemn you. Go now and leave your life of sin.)

Chapter 10: Go for Fresh Air
- Luke 15:11–32 (prodigal son: sleeping in the barn with the pigs)
- Mark 12:31 (Love the Lord Your God with all your heart, soul and mind. That's the first. ....)
- Matthew 19:16–30 (the rich young prince who was told to sell off what he had)
- John 20:24–29 (Jesus's response to doubting Thomas in that upper room)

Chapter 11: More Than Enough
- John 20:28, Romans 1:2–4, 1 John 4:23 (Jesus was equal parts human and divine)

Chapter 12: The Voice of the Shepherd
- Matthew 25:35–40 (I think this how God sees us when we give our best attempts to love God, love others; seek Him first)
- John 20:24–29 (like Jesus invited Thomas when they were together in the upper room)
- John 16:33 (this life won't be easy, that we will have our share of troubles)
- 1 Corinthians 1:9 ("God is faithful, who has called you into fellowship with His Son, Jesus Christ our Lord.")

About the Author

If the story of Jonah and the whale sounds a little fishy to you, don't worry, it did to Kevin too. If you've ever scratched your head when Jesus said, "Whoever believes in me will do the works I have been doing, and they will do even greater things" (John 14:12, NIV), likewise you are in good company.

Kevin never planned on being a writer, moving to Minnesota, coaching women's gymnastics, or for that matter most of his adventures. But part of his story is to point out how, for all of us, God takes those seemingly random experiences and weaves them together for His purpose.

Kevin did move back to Virginia where he enjoys time with family, friends, and his dog, Buddy. He is currently working on his next book. Additionally, he speaks with groups, performs voiceover work, and hosts a podcast. One of his favorite activities is participating in local theater via Logos Theatricus. They are a nonprofit theater group performing plays to raise money for local charities. Most recently the group raised funds for a ministry working with the homeless in southwest Virginia.

If you would like to have Kevin come speak to your group you can reach out via the contact page at www.hizworks.com.